AURELIUS
THE UNKNOWN

MARCUS AURELIUS COMPLETE WORKS 2
ANECDOTES, LECTURES, & LETTERS

STOICISM IN PLAIN ENGLISH

DR CHUCK CHAKRAPANI
THE STOIC GYM PUBLICATIONS

D1546494

Stoic Gym Publications
www.thestoicgym.com

Stoic Foundations/Chuck Chakrapani. —1st ed.
ISBNs:
Print: 978-0-920219-60-7
ePub: 978-0-920219-61-4
Mobi: 978-0-920219-62-1
PDF: 978-0-920219-63-8

18 19 20 21 22 23 24 25 26   1 2 3 4 5 6 7 8 9 0

Contents

Aurelius the Unknown

This is the second of two books covering the complete works of Marcus Aurelius in plain English.

The word "unknown" in the title alludes to the fact these are lesser-known parts of Marcus Aurelius' works. Almost everyone who has heard of Marcus Aurelius knows he was a Roman Emperor who wrote the Stoic classic, *Meditations*. But what about his other works?

What about anecdotes about his life? What about the letters he wrote? What about the speeches he made?

These materials are not widely available. Eighty-five of Marcus' letters to his teacher Fronto are preserved. The only complete English translation of these letters commonly available is a century old,[1] although there are some partial translations.[2] [3] [4]

Those who are curious to understand Marcus Aurelius the man (as opposed to Marcus Aurelius the philosopher-king) must rely almost completely on someone else's interpretation.

This book tries to remedy that.

1

Probably for the first time in one hundred years, we present the complete works of Marcus Aurelius in plain English.

PART 1

Anecdotes: Marcus as Remembered by Others

Unlike formal writings and speeches, a person's reactions to life's situations are mostly uncensored and unedited. They are drawn from the memories of those who know the person, even if their recollection is flawed. For this reason alone, nothing makes a person come alive more than the way they react to things as they go about living their daily lives.

Some of these anecdotes may be less than authentic. Occasionally, there may be an anecdote or two that might seem out of line with what we know of Marcus Aurelius' character. There could be anecdotes that are made up by others. Yet, collectively, they can add depth to our understanding of Marcus, the man.

1. Making his sister equal to her husband

Everything Marcus Aurelius inherited from his father, he gave to his sister. When his mother asked him to share the inheritance equally with his sister, he replied that he was content with being his grandfather's heir.

He further suggested that his mother, too, if she was willing, should give her property to his sister so she might be equal to her husband.

2. Marcus, the reluctant royal

When Marcus learned he had been adopted by Emperor Hadrian, he was more embarrassed than pleased. When he was asked to move to Hadrian 's private residence, he left his mother's house with regret.

When asked why he took it so hard, he replied:

One cannot separate evil from sovereign power.

3. Rulers should be philosophers

Marcus very frequently repeated this saying of Plato:

Well was it for states, if either philosophers were rulers or rulers philosophers.

4. Use people's specific talents

If anyone did anything excellent, Marcus praised them and used their talents for that purpose. But he did not expect other things from them. Marcus said:

> It is impossible to make human beings exactly what one wants them to be. We must use them as they are for any service in which they can be useful for the common good.

5. Take advice from the wise

Before doing anything, whether it was a military or civil affair, Marcus always consulted the chief staff of the state. In fact, this was his favourite saying:

> It is more sensible that I follow the advice of my many wise friends than my many wise friends follow what I would like.

6. Opposition to all blood sports

Marcus was, by nature, opposed to all bloodshed. When requested to allow a lion trained to eat a human being into the arena, he refused to look at it himself and did not allow the trainer to continue. When people protested, Marcus said:

> The trainer had done nothing to deserve freedom.

7. If you want to be rid of the wife, give back the dowry

People suggested⁵ to Marcus that he should divorce his wife, if not kill her. He said,

If I get rid of my wife, I must also give back the dowry.

What did he mean by dowry, unless it was his Empire, which he had received when his father-in-law adopted him according to Hadrian's wish?

8. Physical violence is not the only violence

Marcianus:

I have not been violent.

Caesar [Marcus]:

Do you think you are violent only if you physically hurt someone? It is also violence when you demand someone to give back what you think he owes you when it is not legally yours. It is not consistent with your modesty, dignity, or loyalty to the state to ask for anything, except legally.

9. A philosopher is a physician

Marcus said to Peitholaus that he had but one physician and he was a free man. He went on to say repeatedly about me [the original author is unknown] that I was the first of physicians and the only philosopher.

10. No flattery, no fear

The combat was tough, and the soldiers scored a big victory. Yet, Marcus refused to reward them by saying this:

> *The more they received beyond their fixed pay, the more they would extract from their parents and relatives. Only God could judge matters of his sovereignty.*

He ruled with such wisdom and self- command that, although he was engaged in many great wars, he never moved away from what was right. He did not say anything to flatter anyone. Neither did he do anything because he was afraid.

11. Acting compassionately

Athenians brought a case against Herodes.[6] Herodes was frantic. His judgment was confused, and he wanted to die. Feeling angry and desperate, he had a go at the emperor.

As you would expect from someone who is practised in speaking – but defiant and uncontrolled – he said, "This all comes down to my friendship with Lucius, whom you sent to me. In judging me, you gratify your wife and your three-year-old child."

But when Bassaeus, who had the power of capital punishment, threatened Herodes with death, he said, "My fine fellow, an old man has little more to fear," and he left the court even before his time for speaking was up.

In this trial, Marcus behaved in line with his philosophical doctrines. He did not frown or roll his eyes, as even an arbitrator might have done. Instead, he turned to the Athenians and said,

> *Make your case, people of Athens, even though Herodes doesn't want to hear it.*

He listened to their case. He was secretly saddened at many points when the complaints of the Athenian Assembly were read to him. The complaints openly attacked Herodes for trying to win over the governors of Greece with honeyed words. He even cried out, "O bitter honey!" and, "Happy that they perish in pestilence!" He was deeply moved by what he heard and was brought to tears in public.

The Athenians also complained about Marcus' freedmen. Marcus focused his anger on the freedmen, yet he punished them with maximum leniency, as he himself put it. He spared Alcimedon from punishment because of his recent tragedy with his children, which Marcus thought was punishment enough.

Thus, Marcus acted on this occasion in a way worthy of philosophers.

12. Praying for rain

When Marcus' army was dying of thirst, he raised both hands to heaven and prayed:

> *With these hands – with which I have taken away no life*
> *– I beg you, the Giver of Life.*

God was so moved by his prayer that rain started coming down from a clear sky.

---

13. More useless than Marcomanni

On his way to Egypt, Marcus was crossing Palestine. Along the way, he encountered some unsavoury and turbulent Jews. He is said to have cried out,

> *O Marcomanni! O Quadi! O Sarmatians! At last, I have*
> *found others more useless than you.*

---

14. All in the family

When Marcus was preparing for war against Cassius, barbarians offered him their services. But he refused to accept them saying,

> *The barbarians must not know the troubles being stirred*
> *up between Romans.*

15. Be kind to your enemies

When Cassius' head (who revolted against Marcus Aurelius) was brought to him, Marcus was not proud and did not gloat.

Instead, he was sorry that he was robbed of the opportunity to be compassionate. With tearful eyes, he said, given the opportunity, he would have pointed out the benefits Cassius had received from him and would have spared his life.

Someone objected to this and said it was all Marcus' fault to have shown compassion in the past. Because he forgave his enemies and their children and relatives, they all banded together to throw Marcus out and said,

What if he had been successful?

Marcus replied,

My worship of the gods is not such, my life is not such,
that he could have been successful.

He then said all the emperors who had been killed had deserved their fate. No good Emperor had been easily thrown out or killed. Nero and Caligula had earned their deaths. Otho and Vitellius should not have been emperors in the first place. He felt the same way about Galba because he said,

Greed is the most hateful of all faults in an emperor. Rebels could never overcome Augustus, Trajan, or Hadrian or his own father. Even though they were many, they had

been crushed against the wish, or without the knowledge of, the reigning emperor.

However, Marcus asked the Senate not to be too severe on those who were involved in the rebellion and that no senator be put to death during his reign. This won him everyone's admiration.

16. The emperor's compassion

Aristides, the founder of Smyrna, was distressed by the devastation of his city by earthquakes. When he described the destruction to Marcus, he was so moved by it that he kept sighing repeatedly. When he came to the part which described the "breezes blowing over a city of desolation," Marcus even let tears fall upon the writing and granted the restoration of the city as suggested by Aristides.

It also so happened that Aristides had already met with Marcus in Ionia when they were attending the lectures of the Athenian Damianus. The emperor had already been in Smyrna for three days by then.

Even though Aristides was not known to Marcus personally then, he requested the Quintilii to see to it that Aristedes was not passed over unnoticed in the imperial reception. They said they had not seen him; otherwise, they would not have failed to introduce him to the emperor.

The next day, they both arrived acting as bodyguards to Aristides. The emperor asked,

Why have you been so slow in letting me see you?

Aristides replied,

O King, a professional problem came up. My mind was so engaged in the problem that I felt I should not detach myself from its inquiry.

Charmed by this man's character, his extreme simplicity and diligence, the emperor asked,

When shall I hear from you?

Aristides said,

If you want me to meet me tomorrow, suggest the topic of discussion today. I don't spit out what comes to my mind; I speak precisely. Please grant, O King, that my pupils can also attend the meeting.

Marcus replied,

Certainly; it's open for everyone.

Aristides:

Permit them, O King, to cheer and applaud as loudly as they can.

With a smile on his face, Marcus said,

That depends on you.

17. The emperor's generosity

When he returned to Rome, Marcus addressed his people. He mentioned, among other things, that he had been away for many years.

They shouted, "Eight!" and indicated this with their fingers that they might get so many pieces of gold for a congiarium (a vessel containing one congius, equal to six sextarii.)

The emperor smiled and repeated, "Yes, eight," and afterwards, he distributed 200 drachmas to each one – the largest sum they ever received.

18. Everything belongs to the people

Emperor Marcus Aurelius had the power to demand of the Senate money from the public treasury. Yet he did not demand it, but requested it and said that everything, including the money, belonged to the Senate and the people. He told the Senate,

We don't own anything; even our houses are not our own.

19. Never stop learning

The emperor was an eager disciple of Sextus (a philosopher from Boeotia). Marcus often visited his house and was found in his company.

Lucius, who had just come from Rome, asked the emperor whom he had met on the way, where he was going, and for what purpose. Marcus replied,

> It is good even for an old man to learn. I'm now on my way to Sextus, the philosopher, to learn what I yet do not know.

Lucius raised his hands to heaven and said,

> O, Zeus, the king of the Romans in his old age takes up his tablets and goes to school. But my king, Alexander, died before he was thirty-two!

20. Marcus' last days

When Marcus' health started failing, he sent for his son. Marcus told him not to neglect the ongoing war because it would seem he was betraying the State.

However, when his son told him that his first care was for his health, Marcus let his son do as he wished but requested him not to leave right away but to wait for a few more days.

Then, Marcus stopped eating and drinking, hoping to die. On the sixth day, he called for his friends. He made fun of earthly things and said that death was nothing.

Why weep for me? Why not think about the pestilence and the death that awaits us all?

When they tried to retreat and sighed, he said,

If you now dismiss me, I give you my farewell and lead the way for you.

When they asked to whom he commended his son, he said,

To you, if he is worthy, and to the immortal gods.

On the seventh day, he grew worse. He allowed only his son to see him and yet dismissed him at once, so he may not be infected as well. After his son left, he veiled his head as if he was asleep, but that night he passed away.

21a. The tour's disastrous work

When Marcus was seriously ill with no hope of recovering, he would often cry out in his illness this verse from the tragedy,

Such is the tour's disastrous work!

21b. Go to the rising sun

When Marcus Aurelius was near his death, the tribute asked him for the watchword. He replied,

Go to the rising sun. I am setting.

PART 2

Speeches: Marcus' Public Addresses

Only very few of Marcus Aurelius' speeches have survived. The authenticity of even these are open to question.

The first speech in this chapter was reported by Dio Cassius who was twenty years old when this speech was delivered. He lived in Rome and later held a high office in the state. According to Dio Cassius, Marcus read this address to the soldiers on the rebellion of Avidius Cassius. Because it was a written address, it was more likely to have been preserved verbatim. While the speech appears authentic in style and content, it is possible that it could have been composed by a skilful imitator.

The second speech is a plea to the senators not to harm the relatives of Cassius, who rebelled against Marcus and lost. According to C.R. Haines, the speech is also in keeping with the artificial and rhetorical style of Dio Cassius. There is "dignity and restraint, not altogether unworthy of the occasion, noticeable throughout."

Yet it appears too short for such an occasion. It is possible that it was shortened by Joannes Xiphilinus, the Byzantine historian who lived in Constantinople during the latter half of the 11th century CE, who summarised Dio Cassius.

The third speech is addressed to his close friends and relatives. Here, Marcus, nearing his death, asks them to guide his son who will succeed him as the emperor.

The fourth speech is, in fact, a letter sent by Marcus to the Common Assembly of Asia. (It is included in this section because it is not a personal letter but more of a royal pronouncement.)

Here, Marcus forbids Greek cities from raging against Christians. This letter is of particular significance because Marcus had been accused – not based on any real evidence – of persecuting Christians. This letter shows that, far from persecuting Christians, Marcus was defending them. This was written when he was the subordinate ruler with Pius, either by himself or in conjuction with Pius.

1. To his soldiers (on being forgiven)

In April 175, Avidius Cassius, governor of Syria, declared himself emperor following rumors that Marcus Aurelius had died. He was accepted as emperor by Syria, Judea and Egypt. Even when Cassius learned that Marcus was still alive, he continued his rebellion.

Marcus learned of the revolt by Cassius from Verus, the governor of Cappadocia. He kept it a secret for a while, but because his soldiers were quite disturbed by the rumor and were freely discussing it, he decided to call them together and read the following speech.

O, fellow soldiers, I have not come before you to show my resentment and grief. Doesn't the god who allowed this to happen have the right to do whatever he pleases? Yet those who face misfortune without deserving it cannot but mourn their fate. That's what I am facing now.

Surely, it is a terrible thing for us to be engaged in wars upon wars.

Surely, it is shocking to be involved in civil wars.

Surely, it is more terrible and more shocking that there is no faith to be found among us. The person who has been plotting against me is the one who is most dear to me. I have done nothing wrong and have not misbehaved, yet I have been forced into a conflict against my will.

What morality can be thought of as safe, and what friendship can be thought of as secure, when you see this has happened to me? Is not faith utterly destroyed, and hope along with it?

Yet, if it was only a matter of danger to me, it might not have mattered. After all, I was not born immortal. But now people have defected and there is a revolt; war comes to all of us equally.

If it were possible, I would have invited Cassius to argue his case before you and before the Senate. If I thought it was for the common good, I would have, willingly and without contest, made way for him to assume supreme power.

It is only in the public interest I face hard work and danger and I have spent so much time here away from Italy. I am an old man and ailing. I am unable to eat without pain or to sleep without care.

Cassius would never agree to meet me for this purpose. How could he have faith in me, when he was so unfaithful to me?

Therefore, my fellow soldiers, you must be of good cheer. As far as I can see, Cicilians, Syrians, Jews, and Egyptians have never been a match for you; they never will be, even if they were thousands of times more numerous than you, but they are less.

Cassius is of little importance in the current crisis, alhough he has been reputed to be a good commander, and he has many campaigns to his credit. An eagle at the head of jackdaws is not a formidable enemy; neither is a lion at the head of fawns. It was you, not Cassius, who brought the Arabian War and the great Parthian War to successful ends.

Even if he has distinghuished himself by his Parthian campaigns, you have Verus as well. Verus may have won less often, but was far more victorious and made greater gains.

Perhaps even now, learning that I am alive, Cassius has repented his action, and said it was only because he thought I was dead that he acted this way! But if he still maintains his opposition, he will no doubt think differently once he learns that we are marching against him, because of his dread of you and his reverence for me.

In any case, I have but one fear. Let me tell you the whole truth. Either he would take his own life from the shame of facing us or someone would kill him, knowing that I shall come and fight against him.

Great is the price of war and of victory, and I will be deprived of the prize that no one has ever won.

And what's that?

To forgive the man who has done wrong and still be a friend to the person who trampled your friendship with his foot; to continue to be faithful to the person who has broken faith.

Perhaps what I say may seem incredible to you. But don't doubt it. All that is good has not completely disappeared from among people, but there is still a trace of unspoiled virtue.

If any of you doubt it, I am even more keen for you to see with your own eyes what no man now believes could be done.

This would be the only thing I could get from my present troubles if I could bring the matter to an honourable conclusion, and show to all world that you can use the right principles even when dealing with a civil war.

2. To the Senate (sent for reading)

Regarding how to deal with Cassius, Marcus sent the following speech to be read to the Senate. Here, Marcus pleads with the Senate not to harm Cassius and not to harm his family in any way.

Conscript Fathers, in return for your congratulations on our victory, you have my son-in-law Pompeianus as consul. His mature years should have been rewarded with a consulship long ago, but other brave men had prior claims for recognition from the state.

Now, regarding the rebellion of Cassius, Conscript Fathers, I beg you and plead with you to put aside all thoughts of severity. Safeguard my – rather your – humanity and forgiveness.

> *Let no single person be put to death by the Senate.*
>
> *Let no Senator be punished.*
>
> *Let the blood of no man of noble birth be spilled.*
>
> *Let the exiles return.*
>
> *Let the forbidden recover their properties.*

If only I could recall those already condemned!

Revenge for his own wrongs never sits well on an emperor. The more it is deserved, the more severe it seems. So, you must pardon the sons of Avidius Cassius, his son-in-law, and his wife.

But why do I say "pardon," since *they* have done nothing wrong?

Let them live on their patrimony, proportionately divided. Let them enjoy their gold, their silver, and their clothes. Let them be left in peace; let them be free to come and go as they please. Let them bear witness among all people everywhere to my humanity and to yours.

This is not any great clemency, O Conscript Fathers, to pardon the children and wives of the condemned.

But what I ask of you is that you shield the accomplices of Cassius among senators or knights from death, restriction, imprisonment, disrespect, hatred, and in fact, from all injury. Grant this glory to my reign. In a rebellion, death should overtake only those who have fallen in the revolt.

3. To the Common Assembly of Asia (about our religion)

Here, Marcus Aurelius, subordinate emperor at that time, speaks out against persecuting Christians.

The Emperor Caesar Marcus Aurelius Antoninus Augustus [Arminius], Supreme Pontiff, in the fifteenth year of his tribuneship, consul for the third time, Father of the Fatherland, to the Common Assembly of Asia. Greetings.

Gods are much more concerned about punishing those who refuse to worship them than you are. I am confident that the gods themselves would see to it that such offenders do not escape. But by harassing them and accusing them of being atheists, you harden them, and they hold to their conviction even more strongly. They would rather be accused and die for their God than live. As a result, they come off even more triumphant when they give up their life than agree to your demands.

I believe it is not wrong on my part to remind you of the past and present earthquakes. Whenever they happen, you despair, yet you contrast their faith and conduct with yours.

As a matter of fact, they show more outspoken confidence in their god. You, on the other hand, with your obvious ignorance, neglect all other gods and as well as the worship of the everlasting one. When Christians worship him, you harass and persecute them to death.

On behalf of such people, many provincial governors have written to our idolized father. He has asked that such people not be molested, unless they are working against the Roman government. Many have also given me information about those people. I have replied to them according to my father's view.

If anyone continues to cause trouble to those people for being what they are, let the accused be set free, even if they are charged. Instead, let the person who brought the charge be held accountable.

Published at Ephesus in the Common Assembly of Asia.

4. To his friends and relatives (last request)

When he was about to die, Marcus invited as many of his friends and relatives as were available and set his son Commodus before them. Then he raised himself gently from his straw mattress bed and spoke these words.

It is not surprising that you are grief-stricken from seeing me in this state. It is natural for humans to pity the misfortunes of their kin. The disasters that happen in front of our own eyes call for greater compassion. But I think that something even more will be forthcoming from you to me. The awareness of how I feel towards you has led me to hope for a compensation of goodwill from you.

Now is the time both for you and me to learn that I have not lavished love and esteem on you for nothing over all these years. And for you to show your gratitude to prove that you are aware of the benefits you have received.

You see my son here, whose upbringing has been in your hands, is just becoming an adult[7]. Like a ship caught in a storm and breakers, he needs those who will guide the helm. Otherwise, because of his lack of experience with the right course, he would crash upon the rocks of bad habits. Therefore, you will be many fathers to him in my place, his one father, taking care of him and giving him the best advice.

No wealth can ever compensate for uncontrollable tyranny. No bodyguard is strong enough to protect the ruler, unless he has the goodwill of the people he rules. Such rulers complete a long course of sovereignty, not by instilling fear in their citizens, or by cruelty, but by love and by their goodness.

After all, it is not those who serve as slaves under compulsion but those who are obedient from persuasion and those who are above suspicion who continue doing the right thing without a veil of flattery. They show no restlessness, unless driven to it by violence and outrage. It is difficult to check and put a proper limit to our desires when power becomes the master.

By giving my son such advice and reminding him what he hears now with his own ears, you will make him the best of kings – both for yourselves and for all mankind. You will do my memory the greatest service, and only this way you can make it immortal.

PART 3

Letters: Marcus in Love?

It was a widespread practice in old days to reuse parchment pages of a book by washing what was already on it and writing something new over it. Such recycled parchment pages are called palimpsests. This was economical in terms of parchment use, but it means we have lost many classical books this way.

About 200 years ago, an Italian cardinal and philologist Angelo Mai came across a palimpsest codex (a codex is a book as opposed to a scroll) in the Ambrosian Library in Milan, of which he was the custodian.

Of particular interest to us is a set of letters from Marcus to his rhetoric teacher, Fronto. Three years later, in 1818, Angelo Mai was transferred to the Vatican library. By a surprising coincidence, he found another section of the same palimpsest there.

The main challenge of course was to read the erased text below the newer text. Mai was able to do this by using chemicals. He undertook this challenging task and published the text in 1815 and then a more complete version in 1823.[8]

It took nearly another century for this to be translated into English. In 1919-20, Loeb Classical Library published Charles R. Haines' translation in two volumes.

Since then, there has been no complete translation of Fronto's letters; although, as mentioned in the Preface, there have been a few partial translations.

Of all these translations with commentaries, Amy Richlin's Marcus Aurelius in Love *is the most provocative (not so much the translation itself, but her commentary and interpretation). The letters of Marcus Aurelius to Fronto contain several expressions, such as the following:*

- I am passionately in love with you. (Letter 3)
- Goodbye, breath of my life. Should I not burn with love of you, when you have written me what you have! What shall I do? I cannot stop. (Letter 3)
- ... worn out with such constant and consuming desire for you. (Letter 5)
- My chief joy, sweetest of masters. (Letter 8)
- What more can I say except that I love you as you deserve? (Letter 11)
- Let your love be a measure of your longing for me. (Letter 32)
- What else could I do, when I admired the whole man, loved the whole man so much? (Letter 29)
- What shall I say when whatever I say isn't enough? Goodbye my desire, my light, my delight. (Letter 35)
- My longing for you bubbles and overflows and foams my heart. (Letter 36)

- I imagine seeing you hugging me tightly and kissing me many times affectionately. (Letter 86)

Such expressions would be clearly thought of as expressions of romantic love if they were written today. Amy Richlin makes an elaborate case and concludes that Marcus was indeed in love with Fronto and had a physical relationship with him. Based on her reasoning, it is quite plausible that Marcus was in love with Fronto.

Other scholars[9] are not so sure. They point out that many of the "romantic" expressions we find in Marcus-Fronto letters were not uncommon in those days in non-romantic contexts. Marcus is also on record elsewhere as being against pederasty. He describes his brother as being passionately in love with Fronto also. So, it can be argued equally strongly that Marcus was not romantically involved with Fronto.

In any case, this is not my focus here, and I leave this debate to the interested reader.

I consider these letters to be important for a different reason. They were written over an extended period, starting when Marcus was 18 years old and continuing until he was 45. It provides a glimpse of his preoccupations and concerns over this time.

This volume includes all 86 of Marcus' letters to Fronto, although we only have the opening words of some letters. I have not included Fronto's letters to Marcus here. (They are generally much longer, and there are more than one hundred of them; including them would have more than doubled the size of this book.) Those who are interested in Fronto's responses to Marcus are directed to refer to the other sources in the Notes *section.*

1. On speaking what is true

Written around 139 CE, when Marcus was 18 years old.

To my master.

I have received two letters from you at the same time. In one, you reprimand me and point out that I have written a sentence carelessly. In the other, you try to encourage me by praising my efforts.

Yet, I say by my health, by my mother's, and by yours, that I was more pleased with the former letter. As I read it, I cried out again and again, "O how happy I am!"

Someone may say, "Are you so happy for having a teacher to show you how to write more clearly, more concisely and more elegantly?"

No, that is not the reason why I am happy.

What is it then?

It is that I am learning to speak the truth from you.

Speaking the truth is so hard, both for gods and humans. In fact, there's no oracle that speaks the truth without containing some ambiguity, deviousness, or complexity.

The unsuspecting may be caught in this and may interpret the answer according to their wishes and realize its deceptiveness only when it is too late, when the damage is already done. But it is profitable, and clearly customary, to excuse such things as pious fraud and delusion.

On the other hand, your fault-finding or guidance, whichever it is, shows me the way at once without being clever or insincere.

So, I should be grateful to you for this. You teach me before everything to speak the truth as well as to hear the truth.

It is beyond my capacity to repay this double benefit that I received from you. If you don't make any return on the benefits you gave, how can I exchange like with like, except by being obedient?

Even this may be disloyal to me. I prefer that you, because of your excessive care ... since I had those days free, I had the chance ... of doing some good work and making many extracts ... [missing text]

Farewell, my good master, my best of masters. I rejoice that you, the best of orators, have become my friend.

My lady[10] sends her greetings you.

2. On his longing for his teacher

Written around 139/140 CE, when Marcus was 18 or 19 years old.

Greetings, my best of masters.

If you manage to get a little sleep after the restless nights you have been complaining about, do write to me. Above all, take care of your health. Then get rid of the "axe of Tenedos"[11] with which you have been threatening us. Whatever you do, don't give up your intention of pleading legal cases. If you do, everyone else should shut their mouths too.

You say you have composed something in Greek which pleases you more than almost anything else you have written. Aren't you the one who criticized me for writing in Greek?

However, more than ever, I must now write something in Greek. You ask *why*? I want to see whether what I have not learned yet may help me, because what I have learned has let me down.

If you really loved me, you would have sent me that new piece you are so pleased with. Yet, I am reading your work whether you like it or not. It is the only thing that keeps me going.

This is a bloody theme that you have sent me. I have not yet read the extract from Coelius;[12] I won't read it until I figure out the underlying theme myself. But my Caesar speech[13] grips me in its hooked claws. Now, at last, I understand how much work it is to properly shape a few lines and to take time each day to write.

Goodbye, breath of my life. Should I not burn with love of you, when you have written me what you have? What shall I do? I cannot stop.

Last year, it was my lot, at this same place,[14] and at this same time, to be burning with a desire to see my mother. This year it is you who kindle this desire in me.

My lady[15] sends her greetings to you.

3. Your law doesn't scare me

Written around 139 CE, when Marcus was 18 years old.

Hail, best of my masters.

Go on, threaten me as much as you please. Attack me with a variety of arguments. Yet, you'll never drive your lover (meaning me) away. Nor will I say that I love Fronto less often, or love him the less.

You prove with many vigorous arguments that those who are less in love need help and indulgence. So, by God, I am passionately in love with you. The law you lay down doesn't scare me. Non-lovers may see you as forward and superficial, but I will love you as long as I have life and health.

For the rest – the close packing of ideas, the inventive imagination, and the appropriate promotion of your cause – I would hesitate to say you have far outstripped those self-satisfied and challenging Atticists,[16] but I cannot help saying it because I love you. If nothing else, I think lovers should be allowed to enjoy greater joy in the success of their loved ones.

I say we have won, we have won. Is it [two lines missing here] preferable to talk philosophy under a roof rather than under a tree, inside the city than outside its walls, without a lover than with Lais herself sitting at our side or sharing our home? [Some words missing in the previous sentence.] Nor can I get my mind around the thing that needs watching more: the law which *the* orator [seems to refer to Fronto] of our time has laid down about Lysias or my master's [Fronto's] words about Plato.

This I can say without fear: If that Phaedrus of yours ever existed, if he was ever away from Socrates, Socrates never felt for Phaedrus a more passionate longing than I do now for seeing you.

Did I say days? I meant months. Your letter fixed it so one doesn't have to be Dion[17] to love you so much, if he is seized with the love of you.

Farewell, my greatest treasure beneath the sky, my glory. It is enough to have had such a master.

My lady mother sends you her greetings.

4. Marcus' concern for his teacher's health

Written around 139 CE, when Marcus was 18 years old, probably from Naples.

When *you* rest and do what is good for *your health,* then *I* feel better too. Indulge yourself and take it easy. Then I would say that you did the right thing in taking care of your arm.

I, too, have done something today from one o'clock on in bed: I have been successful with nearly all the ten similes.

For the ninth, I call you as my ally and helper, for it did not respond so readily to my efforts in dealing with it. It is the one where the inland lake in the island Aenaria[18] has another island, which is also inhabited. From this, we draw a certain simile.

Farewell, sweetest of souls. My lady greets you[19].

5. Marcus' birthday prayers for his teacher

Written around 140-143 CE, when Marcus was in his early-twenties.

Hail, my best of masters.

I know that on everyone's birthday, his friends offer good wishes for him. But because I love you as myself, I want to offer hearty prayers for myself on this day – your birthday. I therefore call all the gods

- who anywhere in the world provide present and prompt help for people, and
- who anywhere help and show their power in dreams, mysteries, healing, oracles, or any other way.

Depending on what kind of wish it is, I take my stand in the place where the god in charge of that wish can hear me clearly.

So, first, I climb the citadel of the God of Pergamum[20] and beg Aesculapius[21] to bless my master's health and greatly protect it. I then move on to Athens, and clasping Minerva by her knees, I beg and pray that whatever I may learn of letters, it may find its way to me from Fronto's lips.

Now I return to Rome and call on the gods that guard the roads and patrol the seas that every trip I take may be with you by my side, and that I may not be worn out with such constant and consuming desire for you. Lastly, I ask all the guardian gods of all the nations, and the grove itself[22], whose rustling fills the Capitol Hill, to grant us this: to celebrate with you this day, the day in which you were born for me, with you in good health and spirits.

Farewell, my sweetest and dearest of masters. I beseech you, take care of yourself, that when I come, I may see you.

My lady greets you.

6. No one deserues fulfilment of prayers more

Written around 140-143 CE, when Marcus was in his early-twenties.

Hail, my best of masters.

All is well with us when you are praying for us. There is no one who is worthier than you to get from the gods what he asks for. Unless that, when I pray for you, there is no one who deserves more than you to have prayers on your behalf fulfilled.

Farewell, most sweet lord. Greetings to your lady.

7. Distressed by your pain

Written around 140-143 CE, when Marcus was in his early-twenties.

Hail, my best of masters.

How can I study while you are in pain, above all in pain on my account? Shouldn't I, of my own accord, beat myself with every kind of punishment? By Hercules, I deserve it. Who else gave you that pain in your knee which you write was worse last night? Who else if not Centumcellae,[23] not to mention myself?

What am I supposed to do when I cannot see you and I am tormented with such anxiety? Besides, however much I felt like studying, the court cases keep me from it. As those who should know say they take up whole days. Still I send you today's maxims and the day-before-yesterday's theme.

The whole day yesterday we spent on the road. Today, it is hard to find time for anything but the evening maxim.

You ask, *do you sleep, so long at night?* Yes, I can sleep, for I am a great sleeper, but it is as cold in my room that I can scarcely put my hand outside the bedclothes [for the purpose of writing or study].

But this is really what has driven my mind away the most from studying: because I love literature so much, I did you a disservice at the harbor [Centumcellae], as the event showed. And so, farewell to all Catos and Ciceros and Sallusts, as long as you are well and I see you, without our books and in good health.

Farewell, my chief joy, sweetest of masters. My lady greets you. Send me three maxims and some themes.

8. Restraint is better than attacking

Written around 140-143 CE, when Marcus was in his early-twenties.

Aurelius Caesar to his own Fronto. Greetings.

It is a fact. You have often asked me what you could do to please me most. Now is the time. If my love for you can be increased at all, now is the time to do it.

The trial[24] is coming up. It seems that people will not be listening to your eloquence with only goodwill. They will also be watching for your display of anger and animosity.

I don't see anyone else who would dare to warn you about this. Less friendly people would rather see you acting erratically; truer friends would be afraid of looking friendlier to your opponent, if they distract you from accusing him the way you are entitled to. You may be thinking of some particularly choice phrases for that occasion and they cannot rob you of them by asking you not to use them.

So, even if you think of me as an ill-advised advisor or a brash little boy, or too partial to your opponent, I will not hesitate any longer to advise you to do what I think is right.

Why am I saying "advice"? In fact, it is a favor I ask of you and ask of you now. If you grant me the favor, I will be obligated to you forever.

You may ask whether you should not defend yourself in similar language if you are attacked. Yes, people will praise you more if you don't respond, even when attacked. Still, if he attacks you first, they will of course forgive you if you strike back any way you like.

But I have asked him not to start up, and I believe he has agreed. I love both of you, each for his own merits. I don't forget that he[25] was trained in the home of my grandfather[26], Publius Calvisius, but I've been trained by you.

As a result, I am most anxious that this very distasteful business is handled as honorably as possible. I trust my advice appeals to you, so you will approve what I want.

In any case, I would rather fail in getting what I want than fail as a friend by keeping my mouth shut.

Goodbye, my Fronto, dearest and most loving of friends.

9. Keep your personal feelings personal

Written around 140-143 CE, when Marcus was in his early-twenties.

Hail, my dearest Fronto,

I feel grateful to you, my dearest Fronto. You not only didn't reject my advice, but you approved it.

About the strategies you suggest in your very friendly letter, I have this to say. Everything relevant to the case that you are in charge of must be put forward.

Things that are relevant only to your personal feelings, even if they are justified and based on facts, should be left unsaid. This way, you won't damage your credibility in a totally gloomy business or hurt your own self-respect.[27]

Let others do what they like and conduct the case as they will. The only thing that concerns me deeply is that you not say anything that is unworthy of your character, unhelpful to your case and blameworthy to your audience.

Farewell, my dearest, and to me most delightful, Fronto.

10. I cannot wait to see you

Written around 142-143 CE, when Marcus was in his early-twenties.

Hail, my dearest teacher,

Although I am coming to you tomorrow, I cannot bear writing nothing back – even if it is trivial – to a letter so friendly, so delightful, and so elegant, my dearest Fronto.

But what should I love first? What should I feel grateful for first?

Should I first mention that while you were busy with important projects at home and outside, you still made time to see our friend, Julianus?[28] You did this mostly for my sake. I would be ungrateful if I did not recognize this.

But you say that's no big deal. Yes, it is, if you throw in all the rest – your being there for such a long time, having such a long talk about me, or anything else that would make him feel better. You made a sick man feel more comfortable and a friend even friendlier to me.

On top of that, you wrote me the detailed letter of all this. In it, you included the news that I wanted to hear from Julianus himself, the kindest of words, and the healthiest advice!

Why would I try to hide from you what cannot be hidden anyway? In any case, the very fact that you wrote me such a long letter, even though I am going to be there tomorrow, was most satisfying of all to me. I thought myself the most blessed of men.

With this, you have shown me so much and so sweetly how much you think of me and how much trust you have in my friendship. What more can I say except that I love you as you deserve?

But why do I say "as you deserve"? I only wish I could love you as you deserve!

Yes, that's why I am often angry with you when you are away. I get so mad because you make it impossible for me to love you as I would like – that is, for my soul to follow your love to its highest peak.

With regard to Herodes, go on with what you're saying, please. As our friend Quintus[29] says, "succeed with determined persistence." Herodes loves you and I am doing my best there.

Anyone who doesn't love you doesn't see you with his eyes or understand you with his heart. I won't say anything about ears – after all, everyone's ears have passed under the yoke[30] and are slaves to your voice.

To me, today seems longer than a spring day and tonight will seem drearier than a winter night. For I strongly desire to say hello to my Fronto, and above all, I long to put my arms around the writer of these last letters.

I have written this to you in a hurry because Maecianus[31] was rushing me, and your brother[32] needed to get back to you in good time. So please, if you find any mistakes or confused thoughts or shaky writing here, put it down to haste.

Although I desperately love you as a friend, I must not forget to respect you less as my master than I love you as a friend. Goodbye, my dearest Fronto. You are, beyond all things, sweetest to me.

The Sota[33] of Ennius that you sent back to me seems to be on clearer paper, in a more attractive book roll, and in a prettier writing than before. Let Gracchus[34] wait with the barrel of new wine until we get there. There is no risk that Gracchus will ferment[35] along with the wine in the meantime.

Goodbye, ever my sweetest soul.

11. I am grateful to you and I love you

Written around 142-143 CE, when Marcus was in his early-twenties.

His own Caesar to his master,

I don't have to say how pleased I was at reading the speeches of Gracchus. You know it well. It was you who, with your experienced judgment and kind thoughtfulness, encouraged me to read them. So that your book does not come back to you alone with no one to keep it company, I have added this letter.[36]

Goodbye, sweetest of my masters and friendliest of friends. I am going to owe you for whatever I will ever know of literature. I am not so ungrateful as not to recognize what you have given me when you showed me your own notebook[37] and when you didn't stop leading me every day in the right path and "opening my eyes," as they say.

I love you the way you deserve.

12. Be well enough to be with me

Written around 142 or early 143 CE, when Marcus was in his early-twenties.

Marcus Caesar Imperator[38] to my master

What can I possibly say about my rotten luck? What words can I find to blame these extremely hard circumstances which keep me a prisoner here chained by so much worry that doesn't let me run at once to my Fronto, to my most beautiful of souls? Especially at a time when he is so unwell,[39] to hold his hands and, to the extent it is not painful, to give a sensitive foot massage and stimulate it in the bath, and to support him as he walks?

Do you call me a friend – someone who does not drop everything and fly to you in a hurry? I am lamer than you with my timidity—no, my laziness.

As to myself, I am afraid to say something that you may not want to hear. You have tried in every way to keep me from worrying, with your jokes and witty observations, to show that you can put up with all this and stay totally calm.

Where *my* calmness is gone, I don't know – unless it has gone to you in some mysterious way. For mercy's sake, take care and get rid of this terrible illness you have to bear because you are brave, with all kinds of restraint and self-denial. But, to me, it is a truly harsh and most painful trial.

Please write to me right away about which waters[40] you are going to and when, and how comfortable you are now. Put my mind back in my body. Meanwhile, I will carry around your letter with me, despite its sad tone.

Goodbye, my delightful Fronto. Actually, I have to say it more correctly– after all, you always ... [word missing] a lot.

Oh, there are all kinds of gods everywhere; I pray that my Fronto, most delightful and dearest to me, will get well. Let him always be well with a strong, hale and healthy body. Let him be well and be able to be with me.

Most charming of men, be well.

13. In defense of wakefulness

Written around 143 CE, when Marcus was twenty-two years old; written at Baiae.

M. Caesar to his master Fronto. Greetings.

Now, listen to a very few points in favor of wakefulness against sleep. Yet I am guilty of collusion[41] (being really in favor of sleep while pretending to be against it).

I favor sleeping day or night without stopping. I don't desert him (sleep), and he doesn't desert me – we are such cronies. But I hope that my criticism upsets him, and he leaves a little room, giving me a chance at last to burn some midnight oil.

Now for more subtle arguments.

Here is the first one. You may say that I have taken up an easier alternative in accusing sleep than you who have praised it. After all, who cannot easily condemn sleep? Let me counter that argument. What can be easily condemned is hard to praise. What is hard to praise can serve no useful purpose.

But, I will let that go for the time being, as we are staying at Baiae – the endless web of Ulysses.[42] I will take from Ulysses a few things that are relevant here. Surely, he wouldn't have taken twenty years to reach his fatherland or wandered so long about that pool or gone through all the other adventures which make up the *Odyssey*, but for the fact that "sweet sleep seized his weary limbs."[43]

Yet, "on the tenth day, his native soul appeared."[44]
What did sleep do?

> *The evil counsel of my crew prevailed*
>
> *The bag they opened, and forth rushed the winds*
>
> *The fierce gale caught and swept them to the sea*
>
> *Weeping with sorrow, for their native shore.*[45]

What happened again on the island of Trinacria?

> *Nor winds sweet sleep upon mine eyelids shed*
>
> *Eurylochus his crew ill counsel gave.*[46]

Afterwards, when "the Sun god's oxen and fat flocks ...
they killed and flayed ... and burnt the thighs and ate the
flesh,"[47] what did Ulysses do when he woke up?

> *Wailing, I cried to all the gods high,*
>
> *who, ruthless to my ruin, made me sleep.*[48]

However, sleep did not let Ulysses recognize for long
his native land from which he "yearned to see even the
smoke leap upwards."[49]

Let me leave Ulysses for now and consider Aga-
memnon. He was charmed by haste and led many pla-
toons to defeat and collapse. Surely, it all sprang from
sleep and a dream. So, when the poet praises Agamem-
non, what does he say?

> *Let no one see the godlike Agamemnon sleeping.*[50]

Why? What does he think is wrong?

> *Because no councilor should sleep all night long.*[51]

Once a great orator[52] took these words in a strange way.

Now, let's turn to our friend Q. Ennius. You said a dream in his sleep first inspired him to write. But, if he had never woken from his sleep, he would have never told about his dream.

Then there is the shepherd Hesiod who, according to you, became a poet in his sleep. But, in fact, I remember reading this when I was in school:

> When on the swift steed's track he was leading his sheep to the posture,
>
> Hesiod once was met in the way by a bevy of Muses.[53]

You see what this means? That he was *walking* when the Muses meet him.

What do you think of this, being said by its strongest supporter?

> Sweet dreamless sleep, death's counterfeit.[54]

Enough of these trivialities. I wrote this more because of my love for you rather than because I really believed it. Now after strongly abusing sleep, I am off to sleep. For I have spun all this out for you in the evening. I hope sleep will not pay me out.

14. In praise of Cicero

Written around 143 CE, when Marcus was twenty-two years old.

To my master,

Cicero's letter interested me wonderfully well. Brutus had sent his book[55] to Cicero for corrections ...

15. I can see through your ruse

Written around 143 CE, when Marcus was twenty-two years old.

Hail, my deservedly dearest Fronto,

I see through the subtle ruse you came up with out of pure kindness. Since your praise of me would not be credible because of your partiality, you tried to make it credible by throwing in some abuse. How blessed am I! I am worthy of being praised as well as being blamed by my Marcus Cornelius, the greatest of orators, the best of men!

What should I say about your kind, true and loving letter? "True," up to the first part of the letter. But for the rest, where you express your approval of me, "the lover is blind to the faults of his loved one," as some Greek – I think Theophrastus[56] – says. In judging part of my work, you have been nearly blinded by your love.

I do not write well and yet you praise me. Not because I merit it but because you love me so much, sending me so many and so happily-worded assurances. This I value so much and, since you wish it, I *will* be something.

Your letter had the effect of making me realize how much you love me. As for my lack of spirit, I am still nervous and a little bit depressed, in case I said anything in the Senate today which would make me undeserving of having you as my master.

Goodbye, my Fronto, my – what should I say but – best of friends.

16. You are the greatest lover who ever lived

Written around July-August 143 CE, when Marcus was twenty-two years old.

My most honorable consul, Fronto.

I give up, you win. No doubt about it; in loving, you have clearly surpassed all lovers who have ever lived. Take the garland of victory and let the crier publicly announce this victory of yours in front of the tribunal.

> *Marcus Cornelius Fronto, consul, is the winner. He is crowned the champion in the competition Great Friend-ship Games.*

Even though I am defeated, I will not falter or fail in my devotion to you. Yes, you love me more than any man has loved another man while I, though less energetic in loving, will truly love you more than anyone else has ever loved you. In fact, more than you love yourself.

Now my competition will be against Cratia.[57] I'm afraid I can't beat her. After all, in her case, as Plautus[58] says,

> *The rain of love hasn't just soaked her dress with its big raindrops but soaked her very morrow.*

What a letter you have written me! Even the woman who bore me and nursed me never wrote anything so delightful, so honey-sweet. This wasn't due to your mastery of words or your eloquence. If we apply that test, everyone who breathes – not just my mother – would immediately yield to you, as they do.

But I cannot express how your letter—which wasn't just eloquent and learned, but bubbling with so much kindness, overflowing with such affection, shining with so much love—has lifted my heart up to the heavens and inspired it with the most glowing kindness. As Neavius[59] says, it filled my mind with awe-inspiring love.

In your other letter, you pointed out why you were going to delay delivering your speech to the Senate in which you will be praising my Lord.[60] It filled me with so much joy – forgive me if I am too hasty. I couldn't control myself and had to read it aloud to my father![61]

I don't have to tell you how happy it made him since you are aware of his extreme kindness and, of course, the outstanding grace of your letter. This led us to a lengthy conversation about you that was much, much longer than the one you had with your quaestor[62] about me. Your ears must have been burning for quite a while when you were at the forum.

So, my Lord quite approves and loves your reasons for postponing your speech to another day ... [Manuscript breaks off here.]

17. How long it is since I saw you!

Written in 143 CE, when Marcus was twenty-two years old.

To my master,

From 10.30 until now, I have been reading a lot of Cato,[63] and I am writing this to you with the same pen. I say hello to you and ask you how well you are. Oh, how long it has been since I have seen you!

18. Let's talk about human beings as well

Written in August 143 CE, when Marcus was twenty-two years old.

M. Caesar to the most honorable consul, his master.

Three days ago, we heard Polemo[64] declare that we may have a bit of talk about human beings as well. If you would like to know what I think of him, listen.

He seems to me like a hard-working farmer, extremely shrewd, who has covered his farm with only corn-crops and grapevines. There, without question, the harvest is flawless, and the return is rich.

But nowhere in that estate is a Pompey fig tree or Arician greens or a Tarentum rose or a pleasant grove of trees or thick woods of shady plane tree. All for profit rather than for pleasure. You can praise it, but not love it.

Do you think I am being bold and rash in my judgment of a man of such reputation? But when I remember that I am writing to you, I feel that I am not bold enough for your taste. On that point, I am very doubtful – there is a home-grown hendecasyllable[65] for you! So, before I start becoming poetical, let me stop right here.

Goodbye, most missed of men and dearest to your Verus[66], most honorable consul, sweetest master. Goodbye my sweetest soul.

19. I'd even live in Gyara with Faustina[67]

Written in 143 CE, when Marcus was twenty-two years old.

Antoninus Caesar to Marcus Fronto.

How great your goodwill is towards me; this I have known well enough for a long time. But what astonishes me ... best of orators, is that you can find something to say that is new and worthy of your abilities, on such a commonplace and worn-out subject.

But undoubtedly, the mere wish is an immense help towards what you can do well. Nothing could be more effective than your thoughts; nothing could be more complimentary, yet without any sacrifice of good sense, than your expression of them.

I will not be guilty of defrauding you of your legitimate praise for fear of arrogantly praising myself. You have done your duty modestly and well for which, apart from everything, you deserve praise.

But as for revealing your mind to me, it has not done much. For I know well enough that you always will put the most favorable spin on everything I say or do.

Farewell, my Fronto, my very dear friend.

That part of your speech, which you most kindly devoted to honoring Faustina[68], seemed to be as genuine as it was eloquent. To tell you the truth, by God, I would rather live with her in Gyara[69] than in the palace without her.

20. Your eloquence is unsurpassed

Written in mid-August 143 CE, when Marcus was twenty-two years old.

Marcus Caesar to his own consul and master.

Did the ancient Greeks write anything that is so good? Let the experts sort that out. As far as I am concerned, Marcus Porcius'[70] insults are nowhere as perfect as your praises. If anyone can praise my Lord[71] adequately at all, it could only be you.

Such things don't happen these days. It is easier to imitate Pheidas[72], easier to imitate Apelles[73], easier to imitate even Demosthenes[74] or Cato than to imitate this perfect and finished work. I have never heard anything that was so refined, so classical, so polished and so Latin![75]

Oh, I am happy that you have the gift of such eloquence!

Oh, I am happy to be in the hands of such a master!

What reasoned arguments!

What orderly presentation!

What elegance!

What wit!

What grace!

What words!

What brilliance!

What subtlety!

What charm!

What practiced skill!

What everything!

May my life not be well if, someday, a scepter isn't placed in your hand, a tiara on your head, and a judge's bench set up for you. Then the announcer should call us all.

Why do I say "us"? I mean all the learned people and accomplished speakers. You should point to each one of them by your scepter and caution them with your words. I have no fear that I will be so cautioned. I have more than enough reasons for setting foot in your school.[76]

I am writing this to you in a great hurry. Where is the need to write a longer letter when I send you such a kind letter from my Lord? Goodbye, then, the glory of Roman rhetoric, pride of your friends, a man of distinction, most delightful of men, most honorable consul, sweetest teacher!

In the future, be careful about telling so many lies about me, especially in the Senate. This speech of yours is awesome! Oh, if only I could kiss your head at every heading of it! You made absolutely everyone fade into the background. With this speech before us, it is a waste for us to study; it is a waste for us to work; it a waste for us to try harder.

Be well always, sweetest of teachers.

21. It has been so long since I have seen you

Written in 143 CE, when Marcus was twenty-two years old.

Marcus Caesar to the most honorable consul Fronto.

[Several pages of text missing here]....connected by marriage,[77] and not subject to guardianship and placed in a social position in which (as Q. Ennius says),

> *All give foolish counsel, and all for pleasure only.*

Plautus too says on the same subject.

> *Clever flatterers, who with fast-pledged faith*
>
> *take in the trustful; these stand round a king,*
>
> *and what they speak is far from what they think.*

These problems used to affect kings only. But now even the princes have more than enough men, who, as Naevius[78] says,

> *Still flatter with their tongues and still assent*
>
> *and fawn upon them to their heart's content.*

So, my master, I am right in being keen on setting before me one single aim; right in thinking of one man only when I take my pen in hand.

You very kindly ask me for my hexameters[79]. I would have sent them right away, if I had them with me. But my secretary – you know him, I mean Anicetus – did not pack up any work when I set out. He knows my weakness – if I get them, I will burn them, as I usually do.

But, in fact, those old hexameters are not in danger. To tell you the truth, I love them. I pore over them at night because I spend my days in the theatre. Being tired, I make little progress in the evening and, in the morning, I get sleepy.

Still, in the last few days, I have made five notebooks of extracts from sixty volumes. But, when you read *sixty,* don't be too impressed because it included little Atellane mini-farces of Novius and mini-speeches by Scipio.

As you have mentioned your Polemo, don't mention me of Horace again. As far as I am concerned, he is dead and gone, along with Polio.[80]

Goodbye, my dearest, my most beloved friend. Goodbye, my most honorable consul, my sweet master, whom I have not seen these two years. Those who say that it has been two months,[81] they only count days. Will I ever see you?

22. Let your love be a measure of your longing

Written from Naples in late August 143 CE, when Marcus was twenty-two years old.

Marcus Aurelius, to his own consul and teacher. Greetings.

Since I wrote you last, nothing has happened that is worth writing, nothing that would interest you in the least. We have been spending entire days doing the same things: the same theatre, the same boredom, the same longing for you.

Did I say "the same"? No, everyday it is renewed, and it grows. As Laberius,[82] in his own way and in his own peculiar style, says of love

Your love grows as fast as a leek, as firm as a palm tree.

What he says about love, I apply to my longing. I would like to write you a longer letter, but I can't think of anything.

Wait, I just thought of something. We have been listening to some panegyrists[83] here, Greeks of course. They are so amazing that I – who am as far removed from Greek literature as my native Caelian hill from Greece – could still hope that, in comparison with them, I could even equal Theopompous;[84] I hear that he was the most eloquent of all speakers among the Greeks.

So I, practically a boor, have been encouraged by people of undamaged ignorance, as Caecilius[85] says.

Naple's weather is very pleasant, but highly changeable. Every two minutes, it gets colder, warmer, or more scorching.

At first, midnight is warm, like it is at Laurentum; then at dawn, it gets chilly, like it is at Lanuvium; soon, in the quiet of night, dawn, and twilight until sunrise, it is cold – as bad as it gets in Algidus. After that, the morning is sunny, like it is at Tusculum. At noon, it is boiling, as it is at Puteoli. When the sun has gone to its bath in the ocean, the weather becomes more moderate, as it is at Tilbur. It continues to be the same way at evening and when it is time to go to bed until, as Marcus Procius[86] says, "the dead of night falls swiftly down."

But why am I piling up crazy talks like Masurius[87] when I promised that I would write only a few words?

So, goodbye, kindest master, most honorable consul. Let your love be a measure of your longing for me.

23.Celebrating my mother's birthday

Written in August 143 CE, when Marcus was twenty-two years old.

To the most honorable consul and my best master.

I just need this, over and above everything else that signals your affection towards us. You should send Cratia[88] to join us in celebrating my mother's birthday...

24. A youthful prank

Written in August 143 CE, when Marcus was twenty-two years old.

My wrestling master had me by the throat. Do you want to know what the story was?

When my father got home from the vineyards, I went riding as usual. After I had gone some distance, I suddenly came across a flock of sheep right in the middle of the road. There were four dogs and two shepherds and nothing else.

Seeing us, one of the shepherds said to the other: "Keep an eye on those horsemen. They are the kind who usually cause the most trouble."

As soon as I heard this, I spurred my horse and headed straight for the flock. The frightened animals scattered, bleating and running every which way.

The shepherd threw his staff at me, but it landed on the rider behind me, and we fled. So, he who was afraid of losing a lamb ended up losing his staff!

Do you think I am making this up? It really happened. I could write more of that adventure, but here comes my messenger to remind me to take my bath.

Goodbye, my sweetest master, most honored and most unique of men, my joy, my treasure, my delight.

25. It will be my great day, if you come

Written in August 143 CE, when Marcus was twenty-two years old.

The younger Cratia[89], like her mother, calmed our anxiety for a while, or even completely wiped it away. Because you read him often, I thank you on behalf of my mentor, Marcus Porcius.[90]

I am afraid you will never be able to thank me on behalf of Gaius Crispus,[91] because I have dedicated yes, and devoted yes, and delivered my heart and soul yes, to M. Porcius alone. Where do you think this "and" and "yes" come from? From my very enthusiasm.

The day after tomorrow will be my great day, if you are really coming. Goodbye, dearest and most unique of men, sweetest of masters.

On the day of this Senate meeting, it seems more likely that we will be here than go there. But nothing is decided. You come the day after tomorrow. Whatever happens, happens.

Always be well, my soul. My mother says hello to you and your family.

26.So I may see you sooner

Written in 143 CE, when Marcus was twenty-two years old.

When you are away from me, you read Cato. But I, when away from you, listen to lawyers until five o'clock. Oh, this coming night might be the shortest known! I'm so eager not to stay up late, so I may see you sooner.

Goodbye, my sweetest of masters. My mother says hello to you. I'm so tired that I can hardly breathe.

27.You've done me a favor with your kindness

Written in 143 CE, when Marcus was twenty-two years old.

For sure you have done me a favor with your kindness. For that daily call at Lorium,[92] that waiting till late …

28. Your eloquence is worthy of a poet

Written in 143 CE (fall), when Marcus was twenty-two years old.

Marcus Aurelius sends his greetings to his master Fronto.

For sure, I was shameless to give over my writings to be read by such genius, such judgment! For the Lord,[93] my father, I recited a part of your speech, which he had asked me to choose. The words were crying out loud for their author to deliver them. In the end, I was hardly greeted with "worthy of the poet!"

But I won't put off any longer what you with good reason want to hear the most. My Lord was so moved by what he had heard that he was upset he had to go elsewhere on business rather than be in the court where you were to deliver your speech.

He was terribly impressed by the wealth of the content, the excellent range of expression, the clever originality of the arguments, and the skillful structure of the speech. After this, I bet you are asking me what I liked the best. Let me begin here.[94]

> *In matters and cases that are settled in private courts, there is no danger, because verdicts are valid only within the limits of those cases.*
>
> *But, O Emperor, the precedents which are established by your decisions will hold good publicly and forever. Your power and authority is much greater than what is given to*

the Fates. The Fates decide what happens to us as individuals; you, by your decisions about individuals, make these precedents binding on all of us.

Therefore, if this decision of the proconsul is approved by you, you will give magistrates of all provinces a rule for deciding all such cases. What happens then?

Obviously, this: All wills from far off provinces overseas will be brought over to you for a hearing.

A son suspects he has been disinherited. He will demand that his father's will be not opened. A daughter, a grandson, a great-grandson, a brother, a cousin, a paternal uncle, and a maternal uncle will make the same demand. All kinds of relatives will claim this privilege, so they may enjoy possession by virtue of being blood relatives.

In the end, when the case gets to Rome, what happens then? Heirs mentioned in the will set sail while those who were not will be in possession, looking for postponement day after day, looking to delay with all kinds of excuses: It is winter, and the sea is rough, so I can't make it. When winter passes, it is the unpredictable and fickle winds that cause the delay. The spring passes. The summer is hot, and the sun could burn the traveler and make him seasick. The fall follows. Now it is the crop's fault that he's tired and that's his excuse.

Do you think I'm making this up? Didn't it happen in this case?

Where is the defendant who should have been here long ago to plead his case?

He is on his way.

Where exactly on the way?

He is in Asia.

Is he still in Asia?

It's a long journey even when they hurry.

Is it by shipboard, or horseback or imperial mail that he is making such lightening stopovers?

Meanwhile, Caesar, as soon as the trial is fixed, you are asked to grant an extension and it is granted. When the trial is fixed for the second time, a second extension of two months was asked and granted. The two months passed in the middle of last month and several days went by.

Did he come at last? If he has not come, is he at least almost here? If he is not almost here, has he at least left Asia? If he hasn't left, has he at least been thinking about it?

What else is he thinking about except sitting tight on the property of others, plundering the fields, ruining the estate by wasting it? He is not so stupid as to come to Caesar

*and lose his case rather than to stay in Asia and be in
possession.*

*Suppose this rule that the wills of the dead be brought
from overseas provinces to Rome becomes established. The
danger to these wills will be more disgraceful and harsher
than a rule (if there was one) that said the bodies of the
dead be brought to Rome.*

*At least for bodies, there can be no further harm. Burial is
assured by the very dangers associated with travel. Whether it is swallowed by the sea in shipwreck, swept away in a
river, buried by the sands, eaten by wild animals, or picked
apart by birds, the human body is practically buried
whenever it is reduced to nothing.*

*But, when a will goes down in a shipwreck, then all will be
buried: the estate, the household, and the family.*

*There was a time when wills were brought out of the secur-
est temples of the gods, registries, vaults, archives, or back
rooms of temples. But now wills will have to set sail across
the stormy sea along with heavy cargo and a rower's kit.*

*If it becomes necessary to lighten the ship, the next things
thrown overboard will be wills and beans. We also need to
fix an import fee on wills. In time past .... [A page is illegible here.]*

But let's say something about the funeral. The family
would know how to mourn. A freed slave shows his sorrow
one way, a client who is praised mourns another way, and
the friend honored by a legacy laments yet another way.
Why introduce uncertainty and delay over the funeral?
Legacies of all animals are gained immediately after
death: wool from sheep, ivory from elephant, claws from li-
ons, and feathers and plumes from birds. But a man dies,
and his inheritance lies there, it gets put off, left open to
thieves, and is looted.

I think I have copied down the whole thing. What else
could I do, when I admired the whole man, loved the
whole man – bless him – so much?

Goodbye, my master, most eloquent, most learned,
dearest, to me the sweetest, whom I most long for and
miss the most.

The son of Herodes, born today, is dead. Herodes is
overcome with grief. I would like you to write him a
short letter suitable for the occasion.

Always be well.

29.When you're down, so will my spirit

Written probably around 144-145 CE, when Marcus was twenty-three or twenty-four years old.

How do you think I feel when I think how long it is since I have seen you and why I haven't seen you! Perhaps for the next few days, while you nurse yourself back to strength, I still won't see you.

So, when you are down in bed, my spirit will be down too. When, by the grace of God you stand up, my spirit, which is parched with burning, feverish longing for you, will also stand quickly.

Always be well, soul of your Caesar, of your friend, of your student.

30.   You are first in my thoughts

Written probably around 144-145 CE, when Marcus was twenty-three or twenty-four years old.

I did not write you in the morning because I heard you were better, and I was busy with other business. I can't bear to write to you at all unless my mind is clear, at ease and free. Therefore, if the news is correct, please assure me of that. You know what I want and how I deserve it.

Goodbye, my master, you are so rightly first in my thoughts, before all others, on all occasions. See, my master, I'm not sleepy and yet I force myself to sleep so you don't get angry. In any case, you realize that I am writing this in the evening.

31. My longing for you bubbles and overflows

Written probably around 144-145 CE, when Marcus was twenty-three or twenty-four years old.

Marcus Caesar to his master Marcus Fronto. Greetings.

Once I got into the carriage after bidding goodbye to you, we did not have too bad a journey. We got a bit wet in the rain though.

Before reaching our country house, we took a detour to Anagnia, about a mile off the main road, and then we looked around that ancient place. A tiny place to be sure, but one that had many ancient things: temples, and many religious ceremonies. There isn't a corner where you wouldn't find a chapel, shrine, or a temple, also many books written on linen which has some religious significance.

Then, when we came out, on the gate, we found the inscription written twofold: "Flamen,[95] put on the *samentum*." I asked one of the locals what the last word meant. He said that in Hernici[96] language, the word meant the skin of the sacrificial victim, which the priest puts on his peaked cap when he enters the city.

We were glad to learn quite a few other things as well. But we were not glad about one thing: your being away. That was our biggest concern.

Now, when you left us, did you go to the Aurelia[97] or to Campania?[98] Be sure to write and tell me whether you have begun the vintage or whether you have brought a huge number of books to your country house, and yes, this as well – whether you miss me.

And yet this is a stupid question; you don't have to be reminded to do that. Well then, if you do miss me and love me, write to me often, console me and cheer me up. I'd ten times rather run through your letters than through all the vineyards[99] of the Massic and the Gauran Mount.[100]

Those awful clusters from Signia[101] are too nauseous and their berries too bitter – I would rather drink it as wine than as grape juice. Besides, beyond question, it is more agreeable to eat those grapes when they are dried than when they are pulpy. I would much rather stamp them with my feet than chomp them with my teeth. But still, they may be gracious and forgiving and will forgive me for all this teasing.

Goodbye, the most loving, the most delightful, most eloquent of men, and the sweetest master. When you see the wine fermenting in the cask, let it remind you that my longing for you bubbles and overflows and foams my heart.

Always be well.

32. I am tired, hunting and sneezing all day

Written probably around 143-145 CE, when Marcus was twenty-two to twenty-four years old.

Hello, my most revered master.

We are all well.

By cleverly arranging my meals, I worked from 3 am until 8. From the next hour, I puttered around in slippers quite contentedly in my bedroom. Then I put on my boots and army jacket – because we were asked to come so dressed. I went off to pay respects to the Lord.

We set out for the hunt and did daring things. We heard that boar had been captured, but we were not lucky enough to see any. But we climbed a steep hill, and in the afternoon, we returned home. Me, to my books.

I took off my boots and clothes and spent two hours on the couch reading Cato's speech[102] "On the property of Pulchra," and another one in which he indicted a tribune.

"Hey," you cry to your boy, "go as fast as you can and fetch me those speeches from the libraries of Apollo!"[103] It's no use to send for those volumes. They, along with others, have followed me here.

So, you will have to get around the librarian of Tiberius' library,[104] a little bribe if necessary, which he can share with me when I come back to town.

Well, these speeches read, I wrote a little – rather poorly – fit to be dedicated to the water nymphs or to the god of fire.[105] Today, I have been truly unlucky in my writing – definitely a scribble of a hunter or a grape-picker. They make my bedroom ring with their yodel-ing, a noise that is every bit as hateful and tiresome as that of law-courts.

But what did I say? No, I haven't said anything wrong because my master is an orator.

I seem to have caught a cold. Whether from walking around in slippers in the early morning or from writing badly, I don't know. I only know that, as a rule, I am a runny-nosed person, but today, I seem to be doing much worse.

So, I will pour the oil on my head and go off to sleep. Not a drop of it do I intend to pour into my lamp today. I am so tired of riding and sneezing.

Goodbye for my sake, dearest and sweetest of mas-ters, whom I daresay I long to see more than Rome it-self.

33. I love you and you are not here

Written probably around 143-145 CE, when Marcus was twenty-two to twenty-four years old.

Hail, my sweetest of masters.

We are all well. I slept a bit late because of my slight cold, which seems to have calmed down. So, from 5 a.m. to 9 a.m., I partly read Cato's *Agriculture* and partly wrote, not quite as badly as yesterday, heaven forbid!

Then after paying respects to my father, I cleared my throat by sucking honey water as far as the gullet. I will not say that I "gargled," although it is in Novius[106] and in other places as well. After easing my throat, I went off to my father[107] and stood by him as he performed a sacrifice.

Then we went to lunch. What do you think I ate? A little bit of bread, although I saw everyone else gobbling up beans, onions and sardines, big pregnant ones.[108] Then we went to harvest grapes. We sweated and were happy, and as the poet says, "We still left some high-hanging clusters, survivors of the vintage."[109] We came home after 6 o'clock.

I did only a tiny bit of work, even that without any purpose. Then I had a long chat with my little mother as she sat on the bed. My chat with my mom was this:

What do you think my Fronto is doing now?
And what do you think my Cratia[110] is doing?
And about our little Gratia[111], our tiny sparrow?

While we were going on like this, arguing which one us loved which of you more, the gong sounded to inform us that my father had gone to have a bath. So, we had dinner after a bath in the wine press room.

No, I don't mean we bathed in the wine press room, but we had dinner there, after the bath. We had a good time listening to the yokels insulting each other.

After coming back, before I turned over and snored, I got my mask done and gave the dearest of my masters an account of my day. And if I could miss him more, I would not mind wasting away a little bit more.

Goodbye, my Fronto, wherever you are, my honeysweet, my love, my delight. What is it between you and me? I love you and you are not here.

34. What shall I say when nothing is enough?

Written probably around 143-145 CE, when Marcus was twenty-two to twenty-four years old.

Hello, my sweetest of masters.

Finally, the courier is starting. Finally, I can send you my three days' worth of news. But I cannot *say* anything – that's how much breath I spent dictating nearly thirty letters.

Regarding your last opinion about letters, I haven't yet repeated it to my father. But when we come to Rome, God willing, remind me to tell you about this.

But if both you and I are up in the clouds, neither will you remind me, nor will I tell you. And so, we need to plan.

Goodbye my – what shall I say when whatever I say isn't enough? – Goodbye my desire, my light, my delight.

35.It is shameful for bodily disease to outlast mental determination

Written probably around 144-145 CE, when Marcus was twenty-three to twenty-four years old.

To my master. Greetings.

Your brother just now brought me the good news of your arrival. Heaven knows that I long for you to be able to come, if your health would allow it. I hope the sight of you will do something for my health also. "Sweet it is to look into a friend's kind eyes," as, I guess, Euripides would say. You can easily gauge my current condition by my shaky handwriting.

As far as my strength is concerned, it has certainly started to come back. The pain in my chest is pretty much gone. But the ulcer...the trachea? I'm under treatment and taking every care that nothing works against its success.

I feel that my prolonged illness can be made more bearable only by consciousness of unfailing care and strict obedience to the doctors' orders. Besides, it is shameful that a disease of the body should outlast a determination of the mind to return to health.

Goodbye, my most delightful of masters. My mother greets you.

36.   Greet our consul and our lady

Written probably around 144-145 CE, when Marcus was twenty-three to twenty-four years old.

To my master Fronto.

These things at present ... Farewell, my dearest Fronto, my mother greets you. Greet our consul[112] and our lady.

37. I can never love you enough

Written probably around 145-147 CE, when Marcus was twenty-four to twenty-six years old.

To my master.

I can never love you enough; I will sleep.

38.   Remind me

Written probably around 145-147 CE, when Marcus was twenty-four to twenty-six years old.

ANSWER.

Tomorrow, if you remind me, I will state my case for this word.

39-45. Seven letters with only opening words

Written probably around 145-147 CE, when Marcus was twenty-four to twenty-six years old.

Only the opening words of the following seven letters are preserved.

39

To my master,

    I arrived quite strong ...

    40.

To my master,

    I have taken food ....

    41.

To my master,

    If Faustina's[113] courage ....

    42.

To my master,

    Too long anxious ....

    43.

To my master,

    Into the midst of worries ....

    44.

To my master,

    That fatigue of yours ....

    45.

To my master,

    Possible enough for that matter ....

46. I love myself at the thought of seeing you

Written between 145 and147 CE, when Marcus was twenty-four to twenty-six years old.

To my master.

[Text missing.]... In two days from now, if that is best, let's clench our teeth despite everything. As you are recovering from illness, to shorten the journey, wait for us at Caieta.

As it generally happens with those who have in their grasp what they long for, I begin to make light of it. They get carried away, they feel the abundance, and they are overjoyed. For myself, however, I am even disgusted with everything.

My lady mother greets you. I will ask her today to bring Gratia to me.

Even the smoke of one's fatherland[114]

as the Greek poet says.

Goodbye, my all-in-all master. I love myself at the thought of seeing you.

47.I am ecstatic that you can come

Written between 145 and 147 CE, when Marcus was twenty-four to twenty-six years old.

To my master.

Faustina has been feverish today as well and, in fact, I believe I noticed it more today. But, thank God, she makes me feel less anxious by being such a compliant patient.

Of course, if you were able, you would have come. I am ecstatic that you can come now, and my master, promise me that you will.

Goodbye, most delightful of masters.

48. I am in pain because you are in pain

Written from Lorium between 145 and 147 CE, when Marcus was twenty-four to twenty-six years old.

To my master.

   You are indeed playful. But, this letter of yours causes me great anxiety and huge distress, a most acute pain and a burning fever that I have no heart to eat or sleep or even study.[115]

   You would find some comfort in your speech today, but what am I to do? I have been anticipating the pleasure of hearing it but afraid that your visit to Lorium may be delayed. I am in pain because you are in pain.

   Goodbye, my master, whose health makes my health perfect and secure.

49.   If you are better, that is a consolation

Written between 145 and 147 CE, when Marcus was twenty-four to twenty-six years old.

This is how I spent the past few days. My sister[116] was suddenly seized with such pain in her private parts it was awful to see her. My mother, in her hurry, accidentally ran her side against the wall, causing us, as well as herself, great pain. As for myself, when I went to lie down, I spotted a scorpion in my bed.[117] I was able to kill it before lying down in my bed. If you are better, that is a consolation. My mother feels better, thank the gods.

Goodbye, the best and the sweetest of masters. My lady[118] greets you.

50. I am feeling better now

Written between 145 and 147 CE, when Marcus was twenty-four to twenty-six years old.

To my master, greeting.

I think I have gotten through the night without fever. I ate without feeling sick and am doing very well now. Let's see how the night goes. But, my master, by your late anxiety, you can certainly understand my feelings when I learned that you had been seized with pain in the neck.

Goodbye, my most delightful of masters. My mother sends her greetings.

51. When you are distressed, I should be too

Written between 145 and 147 CE, when Marcus was twenty-four to twenty-six years old.

To my master. Greetings.

I cannot help being distressed. When you write to me that your neck was so painful, I don't wish to be, nor should I wish to be, anything but distressed. As for me, thanks to the gods and to your prayers, I bathed today, ate enough, and drank wine with pleasure.

Goodbye, my most delightful of masters. My mother sends her greetings.

52. Our daughter kept us worried

Written between 145 and 147 CE, when Marcus was twenty-four to twenty-six years old.

Caesar to Fronto.

Thank God, we seem to have some hopes of recovery. The diarrhea has stopped, and the fever attacks have gone. But there is still emaciation and still some coughing.

You understand, of course, that I am telling you of our little Faustina[119] who has kept us worried.

Remember to let me know, my master, if your health is improving. I am praying for that with all my heart.

53. Send me a "shouting" subject to work on

Written between 145 and 147 CE, when Marcus was twenty-four to twenty-six years old.

To my master.

I have the whole day free. If you have ever loved me at all, love me today. I ask you, request you, beg you and plead with you to send me a rich subject. In the law court subject you sent me, I found nothing but exclamations.

Goodbye, the best of masters. My lady sends her greetings. I want a subject with shouts of approval. Humor me. Pick out a "shouting" subject.

54. I wish you had sent me what I asked for

Written between 145 and 147 CE, when Marcus was twenty-four to twenty-six years old.

ANSWER.

When did it occur? Was it in Rome? Do you mean that it took place under Domitian at his Alban villa?

Besides, a theme like this will take more time to make it credible than to treat it with the indignation it deserves. It seems to me to be an impossible subject.

I wish you had sent me a subject like the one I had asked for. Let me know the deadline.

55. I am relieved by my daughter's recovery

Written between 145 and 147 CE, when Marcus was twenty-four to twenty-six years old.

To my master, greeting.

My wish is that you keep a happy vintage and the best of health, my master. I am very relieved by the news of my little lady[120] telling me, thank the gods, that she is better.

Goodbye, the most delightful of masters.

56.   I ask your indulgence in judging what I wrote

Written between 145 and 147 CE, when Marcus was twenty-four to twenty-six years old.

To my master.

As far as I am concerned, the writing is finished. So, send me something else to write. My secretary was not at hand to copy out what I wrote. What I wrote was not to my liking, as I was hurried, and your being not well did not help either. So, I will ask your indulgence when I send it tomorrow.

Goodbye, my sweetest of masters. The lady mother sends you her greetings. Let me have the name of the people's tribune against whom Acilius the censor (of whom I wrote) set a mark.

57.I cannot defend both sides of the argument

Written between April 26, 146 and April 16, 147 CE, when Marcus was twenty-five.

To my master.[121]

Gaius Aufidius[122] is putting on airs, praising his own judgment sky-high and saying that – let me not exaggerate here – no one other than him ever came from Umbria to Rome.

Need I say more? He would rather win praise as a judge than as an orator. When I smile, he turns up his nose. He says that anyone can sit yawning beside a judge, but to be a judge is to do noble work. This is meant for me! However, the deal still turned out well. Excellent, I am happy.

Your arrival makes me happy and at the same time worried. Why happy, you don't have to ask. Why I am worried, honest to God, I will confess. It's because, even though I had plenty of time on my hands, I didn't put in even the tiniest bit of work into what you gave me to write.

Ariston's[123] books are treating me well this season but are also making me feel ill. When they teach me a better way, needless to say, they treat me well. But when they show me how much I fall short of this better way, your student blushes and is angry at himself. I am now twenty-five years of age and yet my soul hasn't absorbed these noble principles and purer thinking. So, I punish myself, get angry at myself, become sad, compare myself to others and starve myself. While I am so worried, I put off writing until the next day.

But, I will think of something soon. As an Athenian orator warned a group of his countrymen, "sometimes you have to let the laws sleep," I will make peace with Ariston's works and let them rest for a while.

After reading some of Tully's minor speeches, I will entirely devote myself to your stage poet.[124] However, I can only write on one side or another because when it comes to defending both sides, Ariston, I am sure, will sleep soundly enough to allow me to do that![125]

Goodbye, best and most honored of masters. My lady[126] sends her greetings.

---

58. We are happy because our girls are well

Written probably between 148 and 149 CE, when Marcus was twenty-seven or twenty-eight.

To my master. Greetings.

You tell me you have pain in your groin, my master. When I remember how troubled you are by pain, I feel very anxious. But I comfort myself with the hope that, by the time it took me to get the news, the intensity of your pain would have been brought down by medicine. But since our little girls[127] - we should boast – are quite well, we think we are enjoying the healthiest of weather and the balmy temperature of spring.

Goodbye, the best of my masters.

59. God, please assure us of Fronto's health

Written probably between 148 and 149 CE, when Marcus was twenty-seven or twenty-eight.

ANSWER.

When you write like this to me, I'm sure you are aware that I am most anxious and pray for your health. Please God, quickly assure us.

Goodbye, my most delightful of masters.

60. I will let my Lord know

Written probably between 148 and 149 CE, when Marcus was twenty-seven or twenty-eight.

ANSWER.

I will let my Lord know right away that your health requires that you rest. But please write to him as well.

Goodbye, my best and most delightful of masters.

61. May your birthday keep you healthy

Written probably between 148 and 149 CE, when Marcus was twenty-seven or twenty-eight.

To my master. Greetings.

May your birthday keep you healthy now and strong for all years to come and happy with all your desires coming true. My annual prayer grows more and more complete as my capacity for love increases and the period of our sweetest intercourse lengthens!

Goodbye, my master, most delightful to me. Give Gratia a greeting and your little Gratia a kiss from me.

62.Please advise and guide Themistocles

Written probably between 153 and 154 CE, when Marcus was thirty-two or thirty-three.

To my master.

If, in your province,[128] you come across certain Themistocles who says he knows my philosophy teacher Apollonius, know that he came to Rome this winter. He was brought to my attention by Apollonius, the son, at his father's request.

May I ask you, my master, to make friends with him and to advise him as far as you can? You will, I know, be always most ready to do what is just and proper by all Asians. But guidance and courtesy and all personal politeness, which both honor and conscience allow a proconsul to show his friends, I ask you to freely extend to Themistocles – as long it doesn't harm anyone.

Goodbye, my most delightful of masters. No need to reply.

63. My brother's speech was even better than my father's

Written probably between 153 and 154 CE, when Marcus was thirty-two or thirty-five.

ANSWER.

On my return from my father's banquet, I got your letter. The messenger who brought it was already gone. I am writing this quite late in the evening, so you may read it by tomorrow. It is not surprising that my father's speech should seem to you worthy of the occasion. But my brother's speech of thanks was, in my opinion, more praiseworthy. As you may guess, he had little time to prepare it.

Goodbye, my most delightful of masters. My mother sends her greetings.

64. I was dismayed to read about your illness

Written probably between 154 to 156 CE, when Marcus was thirty-three or thirty-five.

To my master. Greetings.

After your absence, I was longing to see you. What do you think of your danger?[129] For your escape from it, I thank the gods for the second time after reading your letter, which reassures me, so to speak. I was dismayed to read the details of your condition. But, thank the gods, I still have you and, as you promise, will see you shortly. I have good hopes for your continued recovery.

My mother sends her greetings. Goodbye, my most delightful master.

65. Your house and mine are one

Written probably between 154 and 156 CE, when Marcus was thirty-three or thirty-five.

To my master. Greetings.

May you be looked after for us! May your house and mine be looked after – if you consider our feelings, they are but one house! I know well you would have come to us, if you could have walked even with difficulty. But you will come often and join us, gods willing, in keeping all our celebrations.

Goodbye, the most delightful of masters. My mother sends her greetings.

66. We must have faith in the gods

Written probably between 154 and 156 CE, when Marcus was thirty-three or thirty-five.

To my master. Greetings.

You have added to my anxieties, which I hope, you will relieve as soon as possible by curing the pains in the knee and the swelling. As for me, my lady mother's illness gives me no rest. There is, besides, the near approach of Faustina's lying-in. But we must have faith in the gods.

Goodbye, my most delightful of masters. My mother sends her greetings.

67. I'll feel better when your health gets better

Written probably between 154 and 156 CE, when Marcus was thirty-three or thirty-five.

To my master. Greetings.

By this time, in any case, I hope you can send better news because your letter says you were in pain up to the time you wrote. I have dictated this, walking about. The poor condition of my body requires exercise right now. But I will only feel the full benefit of the vintage season when we see your health beginning get better.

Goodbye, my most delightful of masters.

68. When you can walk, we will be delighted to see you

Written probably between 154 and 156 CE, when Marcus was thirty-three or thirty-five.

To my master.

When you are well enough to walk comfortably, then we will also be delighted to see you. May the gods bring that about as soon as possible and may the pain in your foot get better.

Goodbye, my best of masters.

69. I am glad you have seen my daughter

Written probably between 154 and 156 CE, when Marcus was thirty-three or thirty-five.

To my master.

We love Gratia the more for her likeness to you.[130] So, we can understand how our little girl's likeness to both of us endears her to you.[131] I am delighted in every way that you have seen her.

Goodbye, the best of my masters.

70. Our wish: You should be strong and healthy

Written probably between 154 and 156 CE, when Marcus was thirty-three or thirty-five.

To my master.

You know of course what I wish: that you should be healthy and strong from now on; keep this[132] your solemn day and all future ones, for as many years as possible, with us; or, in any case, don't make us anxious on your behalf.

Of course, I guessed right away that there was some such reason for our not seeing you. And I must confess that I am thankful that the cause was such a complaint of your body[133] rather than some other pain.

Besides, though the diarrhea drains your energy for the time being, I believe your bowels have naturally, and to the good of your health, felt the motions of the spring, while others contrive and bring about this by design.

Goodbye, the most delightful of masters. My mother sends her greetings.

71. I am glad to hear what I want to hear

Written probably between 154 and 156 CE, when Marcus was thirty-three or thirty-five.

To my master.

I now learn what I wish first and foremost to hear. I gather from your letter that your fever is gone. Now, my master, as for the sore throat, you can get rid of it by abstinence and we will have better news from you soon.

Goodbye, my most delightful of masters. My mother[134] sends her greetings.

72. I have a serious complaint against you

Lucius Verus to Fronto, written in 161 CE, when Marcus was forty.

To my master. I have a serious complaint against you, my master. Yet the complaint is not as great as my disappointment that, after being separated for so long, I did not hug you or speak to you, although you came to the palace, and that just after I left the lord, my brother. You can be sure that I rebuked my brother for not calling me back. He couldn't deny that he was to blame.

How easy would it have been, pray tell, to let me know that you were coming to see my brother and would like to see me as well? Or, failing that, to have asked me to return so we could have talked.

What? If you sent for me today to your house, won't I set everything aside and run to you? In fact, I am very upset that I couldn't visit you every day. It is the heaviest penalty of our position that I rarely get an opportunity to come to you alone. I should run to you.

Now, at least I plead with you – as I have no leisure yet to hurry to you – to write and tell me how you are. Affairs of the state, however pressing, will not prevent me long enough from seeing you again or expecting you.

Goodbye, my master, to your dearest and kindest Verus.

73. Send me something inspiring to read

Marcus Antoninus as emperor, written in 161 CE, when Marcus was forty.

To my master.

..... [Lines missing]...

I have read some of Coelius and Cicero's speech – by stealth so to speak – definitely in bits and pieces, so closely one after the other that it took my time off relaxation.

Now our daughters are staying with Matilda[135] in the town and they cannot come to us in the evening because of the air quality.

Goodbye, my best of masters. My brother and my daughters[136] with their mother whose ...[text missing] send you their affectionate greetings.

Send me something to read that you think is particularly eloquent, either of your own, or Cato's, Cicero's, Sallust's, Gracchus' or some poet's. I need relaxation, particularly of a kind that the reading of it may inspire me and shake me free from the cares that surround me. Also, if you have any extracts from Lucretius or Ennius, resonant passages if possible, any that gives the stamp of character.

74. I can easily refute Calpurnius

Marcus Antoninus as emperor, written in 161 CE, when Marcus was forty.

To my master.

... My friend, I mean Calpurnius, and I are having a dispute. I can easily refute him in the presence of all and with you too, if you are present as a witness, that Pylades is superior to his master,[137] just as he is more like Apolaustus.[138]

Seriously though, tell your Valerius Antoninus to hand me the petition, that by our reply, the favor of our verdict may take effect. I read your letter with greatest pleasure and my usual admiration.

Farewell, my master, to your Verus sweetest and dearest.

75. I won't tell you, so you won't scold me

Marcus Antoninus as emperor, written in 162 CE, when Marcus was forty-one.

To my master.

I won't put down on paper why we had our holiday in Alsium,[139] so you won't be upset and scold me. On my return to Lorium[140] I found my little lady[141] slightly feverish. The doctor says, if we soon......[Text missing.] If you were well, I should be happier. I hope to see you soon enjoying the use of healthy eyes.

Goodbye, my master.

76. Who knows better than you the demands of duty?

Marcus Antoninus as emperor, written in 162 CE when Marcus was forty-one.

To my master.

I just got your letter and I will enjoy reading shortly. At the moment, I have some business hanging over me that I can hardly avoid. Meanwhile, I will tell you, my master, what you what you want to hear – briefly because I am busy – that our little daughter[142] is better and can run around in her bedroom.

After dictating the above, I read your letter from Alsium at my leisure. While others were dining, I was lying down at eight o'clock, satisfied with a light meal. "Much good has my advice done you," you will say!

Much, my master, for I have complied[143] with your advice. I will read it more often, so I may follow it more often.

But who knows better than you how demanding one's duty can be? But what I request is what you say at the end of your letter – the pain in your hand. If the gods are kind, my master, and grant my prayers, you will not suffer pain since.

Goodbye, my best of masters, man of the warm heart.

77. Gods will grant my prayers because they will be delighted to

Marcus Antoninus as emperor, written in 162 CE, when Marcus was forty-one.

To my master.

A good year, good health, and good fortune – these are things I ask of gods on your birthday, a special day[144] for me. I am confident they will grant my prayers because I asked them to confer their benevolence on someone they themselves consider worthy and would be delighted to help.

You, my master, when other joyous thoughts pass through your mind on your festive day, count those who dearly love you; among them, place your student and my brother at the top of the list. Both of us love you passionately.

Goodbye, my master, may you enjoy unbroken good health with your daughter for many years to come. Your grandchildren[145] and son-in-law be spared to make your happiness complete.

Our Faustina is recovering her health. Our little Antoninus coughs rather less. The occupants of our little nest offer our prayers for you, as far as they are old enough to do so. Next year, the year after, and right into a long old age, most delightful of masters, may you have the best of good health.

I ask you – don't refuse me – not to take the trying journey to Lorium for Cornificia's birthday. God willing, you will see us in Rome a few days from now. But if you love me, spend the coming night in peace and quiet. Don't attend any business no matter how urgent. Grant this to your Antoninus, who asks it with sincerity and concern.

78.My master is now my advocate as well!

Marcus Antoninus as emperor, written in 162 CE, when Marcus was forty-one.

ANSWER to my master.

So, my master will now be advocate as well!

I feel the truth readily in my mind when I have followed the two guides dearest to my heart: right reason and your opinion. God, grant me this: Whatever I do, may I always do it with your favorable endorsement, my master.

You see how late I am writing my reply to you. After consulting with my friends until now, I have carefully collected all points which weighed with us. Now I can write fully to our Lord,[146] and make him our judge here as well. I will I have the confidence in our decision, only when it has been approved by him.

The "speech"[147] in which you have advocated our cause, I will show Faustina right away. I offer her thanks because I had the opportunity to read such a letter from you.

Good master, best of masters, goodbye!

79. It's man's privilege to forgive

Marcus Antoninus as emperor, written in 163 CE, when Marcus was forty-two.

To my master. Greetings.

I have held back from telling you all that had necessarily to be set right, or provided for on time, or quickly fixed or carefully arranged. Make allowance for my principles.

If I have to deal with urgent business, I dealt with what was on hand first. Counting on your good-natured leniency towards me, I have given up writing in the meanwhile. Excuse me for my relying on our love. If I did not describe my actions in detail it is because they were liable to be changed daily, some are doubtful, and all predictions are risky.

Please accept, I pray, such a valid reason for the delay. Why do I write others more often than I do to you, then? To give you a short excuse: if I hadn't done that, they would be angry, but you would forgive; they would give up writing, but you would persist; for them, it is my duty, but for you, it is my love.

Or would you wish me write to you too – unwillingly, grudgingly, and in hurry – because I must rather than I want to? You may ask, why don't I want to?

Because I have done nothing that would make me invite you to share my joy. I confess that I did not want someone so very dear to me, and someone whom I always wish to be happy, a partner in my anxieties that made my days and nights miserable and despair of success. Neither did I want to feel one way and say something else.

Lucius making pretenses to Fronto! From him, I learnt simplicity and the love of truth long before I learned the lesson of polite wording. As a matter of fact, even by long-standing agreement between us, I am eligible for a pardon. In any case, when, despite my repeated requests, you did not write, I was sorry. But, by God, because of our agreement, I wasn't angry.

Finally, why say more, when I don't seem to justify myself as much as to plead with you?

I am at fault, I admit. Against the last person that deserved it, that too I admit. But now you must be better than me.

I have suffered enough punishment: first in being aware of my fault and then, even though face to face I could have won your pardon in a second, I must now, separated as I am by such a distance, be tortured with anxiety for so many intervening months until you get my letter and I get your answer back.

I present to you as petitioners in my favor humanity herself. After all, even to offend is human and it is man's peculiar privilege to forgive....

80. I saw you when I read your letter

Marcus Antoninus as emperor, written in 163 CE, when Marcus was forty-two.

To my master. Greetings.

I saw my sons when you saw them. I saw you too, when I read your letter. I plead with you, my master, continue to love me as you do; love me as much as you love those little ones of ours. I have not yet said all that I wanted to say. Love me as you have loved me.

The extraordinary delightfulness of your letter led me to write this. As to its elegant style, what can I say, except you speak Latin while the rest of us speak neither Latin nor Greek?

Write often to my brother, I pray you. He particularly wants me to get you to do this. His wishes, however, make me unreasonable and demanding. Goodbye, my most delightful of masters. Give my love to your grandson.

81-82. Letters with only the opening words

Marcus Antoninus as emperor, written in 163 CE, when Marcus was forty-two.

Only the opening words of the following two letters remain.

To my master. Greetings.
    I have been unwell, my master ....

To my master. Greetings.
    I hasten to write, my master ....

83. My Lord rests upon your kind letters

Marcus Antoninus as emperor, written in 163 CE, when Marcus was forty-two.

To my master. Greeting.

[Text missing] ... since nothing is more to be relied upon or more readily given, my master, than your kindly take on our services to you.

Write then to my Lord,[148] who promises to write many letters in return, that you have received this message from me. Add also other tokens of your affection and good nature, my master, for he rests upon them. He has every reason to do so.

For the past two days, I had no rest except for the sleep I got at night. So, I have had no time to read your long letter to my lord, but I eagerly look forward to an opportunity to do so tomorrow.

Goodbye, my most delightful of masters. Love to your grandson.

84. This holiday of mine is burdened with state business

Marcus Antoninus as emperor, written in 163 CE, when Marcus was forty-two.

To my master. Greetings.

While enjoying this healthy country air, I feel that I lack one thing – the assurance that you are also enjoying good health, my master. That you make good the defect in my prayer to the gods.

But this holiday of mine burdened with state business is your busy city life still. In a word, I cannot go on with this letter even for a line or two without urgent duties interrupting. I enjoy a rest from them only for a part of the night.

Goodbye, my most delightful of masters.

If you have any selected letters of Cicero, either in full or in extracts, lend them to me. Or tell me what I should read in particular to improve my command of language.

85. My achievements can be made to look as great as you make them seem

Marcus Antoninus as emperor, written in 165 CE, when Marcus was forty-four.

To my master. Greetings.

[Text missing] ... they have added to their letters at the end. However, you can learn what was done after I had set out from the dispatches sent by the commanders who were assigned to it. Our friend Sallustius, now called Fulvianus, will provide you with copies of them.

But that you may also give the reasons for my actions, I will send you my own letters as well, in which what needs to be done is clearly laid out. If you would like some pictures as well, you can get them from Fulvianus.

To put you in touch with what is really happening, I have asked Alvidus Cassius and Martius Verus to write me a memo, which I will send you. From them you will be able to assess the character of the men and their capabilities. But, if you also would like me to write a memo, let me know in what form you would like it and I will follow your instructions.

I am ready to follow any of your suggestions so long as my exploits are set in a bright light by you. Of course, you will overlook my speeches to the Senate and rants to the army. I will also send my negotiations with the enemy. These will be of significant help to you.

One thing I don't wish to point out to you as a student to his master – but offer for your consideration – you should dwell in detail on the causes and early stages of the war, our lack of success in my absence in particular.

Don't be in a hurry to describe my part. It is important to make it clear the vast superiority of the Parthians before my arrival, so the magnitude of my achievements may become clear.

Whether you should only give a sketch of all this, as Thucydides did in his *Narrative of the Fifty Years War*,[149] or go a little more deeply into the subject without expanding on it, as you would upon mine in the sequel, it is for you to decide.

In short, my achievements, whatever their character, are no greater than they actually are. But they can be made to look as great as you would make them seem.[150]

86. My brother would like the transcripts

Marcus Antoninus to Fronto, written in 165 CE.

To my master.

The lord my brother desires that the speeches should be sent to him as soon as possible by me or by you. I prefer that you send them. You may have the copies I sent you readily available. I will get more copies made ... [Text missing] ... without any undue delay, will write me others.

Farewell my sweetest of masters. My love to your grandson.

87. I suffer agony even when a single joint of yours aches

Marcus Antoninus as emperor, written in 165 CE, when Marcus was forty-four.

To my master. Greetings.

I just heard of your misfortune. I suffer agony even when a single joint of yours aches. My master, how do you think I feel when you are suffering heartache?

In my anguish, I could think of nothing other than to ask you to keep safe for me the sweetest of masters, in whom I find a great comfort for this life than you can find from anyone for your sorrow.

I have not written with my own hand because after my bath in the evening, my hand is still trembling. Goodbye, most delightful of masters.

88. It is a father's part to pour out a heart full of love and affection

Marcus Antoninus as emperor, written in 165 CE, when Marcus was forty-four.

To my master.

You are aware, I am sure, my dearest master, even if I keep quiet, how keenly I feel every trouble of yours, no matter how minor. But since you have lost both your wife – beloved through many years – and your sweetest grandson at the same time .... [Text missing.].... and you have known greater miseries than I can dare to console my master with well-tuned words.

It is a father's part to pour out a heart full of love and affection ... Now I will turn to the rest of your letter. I was delighted ... What do you ask, my master? ... what else at all do I more learned either ask of dream of ... [Text missing.]

89. I imagine seeing you hugging me tightly and kissing me

Marcus Antoninus as emperor, written in 166 CE, when Marcus was forty-five.

To my master.

Why should I not picture your joy, my master? To tell the truth, I imagine seeing you hugging me tightly and kissing me many times affectionately ...

PART 4

Who Was Marcus Aurelius?

Marcus, the philosopher-king

Marcus, the author of *Meditations,* ruled the Roman Empire from 160 CE until his death in 180 CE. His empire was the largest the world had ever seen until that time. Yet, he was a philosopher at heart and a reluctant king

Historians judge him as one of the "five good emperors," all of whom ruled the Roman Empire between 69 and 180 CE. Marcus was the last good emperor. Because Marcus he ruled for 20 years, the details of his life are well recorded.

Family background

Marcus Aurelius was born on April 26, 121 CE as Marcus Annius Verus.[151] His family was originally from Ucubi, a small town southeast of Cardoba in Iberian

Baetica. Marcus' family was prominent. His great grandfather was a senator and his grandfather was made a patrician.

Marcus' father, Marcus Annius Verus III, married Domita Lucilla, who was a wealthy woman. Her mother had inherited a vast fortune from her maternal grandmother and from her paternal grandfather by adoption. Among the things she inherited were large brickworks on the outskirts of Rome. The brick factories were very profitable, for this was the time when there was a construction boom in Rome. The family's affluence made them politically influential.

Childhood

Marcus' father died when he was just three years old, in 124 CE, not long after his sister Annia Cornficia Faustina was born in 122 or 123 CE. While his mother did not remarry, she did not spend much time with her son either, as it was the aristocratic custom in those days. Rather, Marcus was mostly looked after by nurses. According to Marcus Aurelius, his mother avoided the ways of the rich, was pious, and followed a simple diet.

The Roman law at that time considered the oldest living male in a household the head of the household. So, after his father died, his paternal grandfather Marcus Annius Verus (along with another person known as Lucius Catilius Severus) raised him.

Marcus was raised in Caelian Hill, in his parents' home. Caelian Hill was an exclusive neighborhood housing many aristocratic villas. Marcus' grandfather owned his own palace near the Lateran Palace, an ancient palace of the Roman Empire. This is where Marcus spent much of his childhood.

Education

Marcus was educated at home, as was the common among aristocrats of the time. In *Meditations*, Marcus thanks Catilius Severus (who shared his upbringing) for encouraging him to avoid public schools.

Marcus' painting teacher, Diogentus, introduced his young protégé to the philosophic way of life. When he was eleven years old, Marcus started adopting the dress and habits of the philosopher at the behest of Diogentus, wearing a coarse cloak and sleeping on the ground, until his mother convinced him to sleep on a bed.

When Marcus was 11 or 12 years old, a new set of tutors – Alexander of Cotiaeum (a well-known Homeric scholar), Trosius Aper, and Tuticius Proculus – were appointed to look after his education.

Royal adoption

Emperor Hadrian, who had no natural-heirs, nearly died of a hemorrhage in 136 CE. While recuperating in his villa at Tivloi, he chose to adopt Lucius Ceionius Commodus, Marcus' intended father-in-law, to ensure succession, against the wishes of everyone.

We are not sure why he chose to do this, but we can assume his intention was to make the then young Marcus eventually the emperor. As a part of the adoption process, Commodus was named Lucius Aelius Caesar, but he was of poor health. After a brief stint on the Danube River, Aelius returned to Rome to address the Senate on January 1, 138 CE. However, the night before the address, he grew ill and died of hemorrhage the following day.

On January 24, Hadrian chose Aurelius Antoninus, the husband of Marcus Aurelius' aunt, as his new successor. Antoninus was adopted on February 25 on the condition that he adopted Marcus Aurelius and Lucius Verus (son of Lucius Aelius) in turn.

Philosophically-inclined Marcus, however, wasn't particularly excited about the prospect of becoming an emperor. It was with reluctance he moved away from his mother's Caelian home to the residence of Emperor Hadrian.

Hadrian continued to groom Marcus to be his successor. When Marcus was 17, Hadrian requested the Senate make Marcus a *quaestor* (a public official with judicial powers), although the minimum age for that position was 24 at that time.

The Senate agreed, and Marcus served under Antoninus, the consul for the year 139 CE. Through it all, Marcus remained true to his character, without getting carried away by all the honors bestowed upon him. He kept his friendships, was as thrifty and careful about his possessions as before, continued to study and practice philosophy and was completely unpretentious as though he was a private citizen.

Hadrian's death

Hadrian continued to be unwell, and his physical condition did not improve. He tried to commit suicide several times but was thwarted by Antoninus.

Hoping to rfecover, Hadrian left Rome and went to the seaside resort of Baiae, on the Campanian coast. When his condition still failed to improve, he decided to ignore the diets ordered by his doctors and started indulging in food and drink. This resulted in his death on July 10, 138 CE.

Antoninus succeeded Hadrian. The succession was peaceful because Antoninus kept the status quo, respecting Hadrian's nominees to the office and acknowledging the privileges of the Senate.

The Grooming of Marcus

Antoninus continued to groom Marcus as the heir apparent. He asked Marcus – and Marcus agreed – to get engaged to Antoninus' daughter Faustina.

Antoninus appointed Marcus as a *seviri,* one of the six knights' commanders at the annual parade on July 15, 139 CE and made him consul when he was just 29 years old. He became the head of the equestrian order and took the name Caesar: Marcus Aelius Aurelius

Verus Caesar. Marcus also joined the priestly colleges at the request of the Senate.

Marcus' developing interest in philosophy

While he was being groomed to be the emperor, Marcus continued his study of philosophy in all seriousness. One of his philosophy teachers was Junius Rusticus, the grandson of Arulenus Rusticus, a Stoic-leaning senator who opposed the tyranny of Domitian. Junius was thus an heir to the tradition of Stoic opposition and he introduced[152] the young Marcus to Stoicism. Junius was highly influential in getting Marcus interested in Stoicism. As Marcus would write later, Rusticus taught him,

> *Not to be sidetracked by my enthusiasm for rhetoric. Not to write treatises on abstract questions, or deliver moralizing little sermons ... To steer clear of oratory, poetry, and belles lettres ["fine writing"].[153]*

When Marcus was about 25, he was influenced by the writings of Ariston of Chios and declared to his rhetoric master Fronto (see his letters earlier in this book) that, in developing arguments, he would be guided by philosophy rather than by rhetoric.

After Marcus assumed the title Caesar, he cautioned himself (as he said much later in his *Meditations*) against becoming an emperor like all Caesars:

> *See that you do not turn into Caesar ... for that can happen.[154]*

At the insistence of Antoninus, Marcus took up residence in the House of Tiberius and adopted "pomp of the court," all under protest. He struggled to reconcile his philosophic bent with the royal conventions expected of him but believed that these two were reconcilable. Years later, he declared:

> *Anywhere you can lead your life, you can lead a right one.*
>
> *Leading a life – so leading a right life – is possible at court.*

But he didn't find it easy all the same, as seen by his later writings.

Marcus' responsibilities

Marcus had minimal responsibilities as a quaestor, such as doing secretarial work for the senators and standing in for Antoninus when he was away.

His responsibilities as a consul, however, were more substantial, as he was being groomed to become the ruler of the Roman Empire.

As one of the two top senior representatives of the Senate, he was expected to chair the Senate meetings, deliver speeches to the Senate, and play a leading role in its administrative functions. He was kept quite busy at this time and complained to his rhetoric master Fronto about his having to "dictate thirty letters" (see elsewhere in this book).

Marcus in love?

When he was about 15 years old, Marcus started studying rhetoric, a required skill for rulers. He had four masters: three in Greek and one in Latin. Marcus' Latin rhetoric master Fronto was reputed to be second only to Cicero, and Marcus loved him deeply.

Marcus' relationship with Fronto was very deep. They exchanged many sentimentally-worded letters (see Marcus' letters earlier in this book). These letters stretch from the time Marcus was 18 years old until he was 45, about which time Fronto died. By today's standards, these letters would be considered romantic in a sexual sense. In fact, Amy Richlin, a classics professor at UCLA, believes they were romantically involved. However, Marcus' other writings indicate he was against pederasty.

Whether Marcus was "in love," as Richlin suggests, or was just deeply friendly with Fronto, we will never know. However, the letters themselves, covering as they do most of Marcus' adult life, are of considerable significance. They provide an insight into Marcus' personal thoughts over the years.

Marcus' concern for others

One of his Greek masters was a rich and distinguished Athenian, Herodes Atticus, who was an opponent of Stoicism. He felt a Stoic would lack feelings and live a sluggish life while Marcus was inclining towards Stoicism. Fronto, the master Marcus loved, did not care much for Herodes Atticus.

Yet, Marcus did not want Herodes to be hurt. When there was a case in which Herodes was up against Fronto, Marcus pleaded with Fronto privately (see his letters) not to attack Herodes, after first requesting of Herodes he not be the aggressor. Although we do not know exactly what the outcome was, this episode describes Marcus' concern for others.

Marcus' marriage

Marcus was made a consul for the second time on January 1, 145 CE. By now, he had been engaged to his first cousin Faustina for seven years. Marrying her was slightly problematic under Roman law, because Faustina was also technically his sister, as Antoninus Pius had adopted Marcus as his son. This meant that Antoninus had to formally release Marcus or Faustina from his parental authority.

Later that year, Marcus married Faustina. Commemorative coins were issued with the heads of the Royal couple to mark the occasion, although Marcus himself made little reference to any of these events in his letters.

Marcus' children

Marcus' wife Faustina gave birth to thirteen children (including two sets of twins), many of whom did not survive. Their first child, Domitia Faustina, was born on November 30, 147 CE.

To celebrate the event, Antoninus Pius gave Marcus the *tribunician*[155] power and the *imperium*[156] on the following day. Domitia turned out to be a sickly child, only to die when she was ten years old.

The twin boys Faustina gave birth to two years later in 149 CE did not survive long either. We are not sure how many of the thirteen children survived past their childhood.

Marcus becomes the emperor

Antoninus Pius' health deteriorated as he aged. By the time he turned seventy, he could barely keep himself straight without stays. He started transferring more and more authority to Marcus and died in 160 CE.

Finally, just before his death, he summoned the imperial counsel and transferred the state to Aurelius and Faustina. Faustina, who was three months pregnant at this time, inherited Antoninus' fortune. Marcus, about to be the emperor, had no need for it.

The Senate planned to confirm Marcus as the sole emperor, but Marcus refused to assume power unless his brother Verus was given equal power. The Senate did not quite favor this, but Marcus was adamant.

Eventually, the Senate gave in to his demand and Marcus became the emperor, sharing the power with Verus. Marcus Aurelius became Imperator Caesar Lucius Aurelius Verus Augustus.

It was the first time Rome was ruled by two emperors at the same time. While in theory Verus shared the power equally, in reality, Marcus had greater authority than Verus. Marcus had shared administrative duties with Antoninus and was *Pontifex Maximus*.[157]

Marcus' early years as the emperor

As soon as Marcus and Verus became emperors, Aurelius' daughter Annia Lucia, then 11 years old, was betrothed to Verus. In the ceremony that followed, Marcus made new provisions to support poor children.

They permitted free speech, and comedy writers, such as Marullus, could poke fun at them without any fear of retribution—an uncommon thing in imperial Rome. They lacked pomp.

All these things made the royal brothers very popular. The early days of Marcus' rule were peaceful, and everything went on smoothly for a while. Marcus found time to pursue his philosophical interests. Things were going so well that, in 161, the emperors issued a coin proclaiming "Happy times" (*Felicitas temporum*).

But this was not to last.

War clouds gather

In the year 161 CE, King Vologases IV of Parthia attacked a client state of Rome, the Kingdom of Armenia. He removed its king and appointed his own. The Governor Severianus of Cappadocia was an experienced military man, and he took it upon himself to fight back but was completely defeated in three days. The Parthian army went on to defeat the Syrian governor's army.

War clouds gathered on other fronts as well: in Britain, in Raetia,[158] and in Upper Germany. The northern frontiers of Marcus' empire were strategically weakened. Marcus, who probably had received no military training, was unprepared. Frontier governors were instructed to avoid confrontation wherever possible.

During the winter of 161-162, a rebellion was developing in Syria, and Verus was sent to direct the Parthian War, while Marcus stayed behind in Rome. During the middle of the Parthian War, Verus took a break to get married to Marcus' daughter, Lucilla, who was not yet fifteen.

The threat of famine

While all this was happening, in the spring of 162, the Tiber River overflowed, flooding large parts of Rome, drowning many animals, and creating famine in the city. Marcus gave his personal attention to the crisis.

The wars continue

The Roman army was successful in capturing the Armenian capital in 163. A new capital was named, and a new king instated. But, during the same year, the Parthians attacked another Roman client state, Osroene (Upper Mesopotamia). In 165, the Roman army moved into Mesopotamia, defeated the Parthians and reinstalled the king who had been removed by the Parthians. The wars continued until 166, when the victorious Verus returned to Rome.

The plague

When Verus returned home, his army brought plague with it. For years, the empire was affected by infection. A pandemic of small pox and measles began spreading as well. Verus died in 169 CE, and it may well have been due to the epidemic.

The disease broke out again in 169, claiming two thousand lives a day in Rome. The mortality rate rose to 25%. An estimated five million people died. One-third of the Roman army was also killed in many areas.

Marcus and the Marcomannic wars

Around the same time, Germanic tribes and other nomadic people started attacking Rome along its northern border, especially along northern Europe (Gaul) and the Danube. The most dangerous of the new invasions was the invasion of Marcomanni of Bohemia (another Roman client state) along with other Germanic tribes.

Marcus Aurelius took charge of the battles and pushed back the attackers. Most of Marcus Aurelius' later years were spent on the battlefields, which is where he wrote his famous notes to himself, now known as *Meditations*.

Cassius revolts against Marcus

In 175, while Marcus was away fighting the invaders in Danube, rumors began to spread that he had died on the battlefield. Governor Avedius Cassius of Syria declared himself emperor and was accepted by Syria, Judea, and Egypt.

Cassius carried on his rebellion even after it had become obvious Marcus was still alive. Verus, the governor of Cappadocia, informed Marcus Aurelius of the revolt. Marcus kept it a secret for a while, but the rumors could not be contained.

This forced Marcus to march east to quash the rebellion. But he did not have to complete the journey. One of his soldiers assassinated Cassius and brought his head to Marcus. Marcus refused to see it.

While Marcus wanted to quell the rebellion, he did not want to harm Cassius if he could avoid it. He had told his troops that he would like

to forgive the man who has done wrong and still be a friend to the person who trampled your friendship with his foot; to continue to be faithful to one who has broken faith.

Death of Faustina

At about the same time, Marcus' wife Faustina the Younger died in the village of Halala in Cappadocia (now in eastern Turkey) due to unknown causes. Although there were rumors that she killed herself to avoid the penalty for conspiring with Alvidius Cassius to overthrow her husband, the charge is almost certainly not true. There were also claims that she was unfaithful to her husband, although there was no definitive evidence.

Marcus delivered a eulogy and honored her memory by establishing a new order of underprivileged girls ("Faustina's girls") to be supported by the State. Marcus did not remarry because he did not want to "burden his children with a step mother." He did however, take the daughter of Faustina's steward as his mistress.

The story of *Meditations* and how it survived

The last decade of Marcus' life was spent mostly in battlefields fighting various invaders and rebels. Marcus, whose soul was steeped in philosophy, had to reconcile his desire for peace with his duty as a king to fight the invaders. In fact, many things he had to do as an emperor were not in line with his philosophical bent.

He detested blood sports, yet he would attend gladiatorial fights because he felt it was his duty to do so. He was a reluctant emperor, yet he marched against Alvidius Cassius because, as the emperor, he could not allow rebellion.

Where there were rumors of his wife's unfaithfulness, he was advised to annul his marriage to Faustina. He replied that if his marriage to Faustina was annulled, he also had to return the dowry, which was the Roman empire, because it was passed to him by her father. During this time, Marcus was also acutely aware of his mortality. He felt he did not have many years left.

At the battlefields he began writing his thoughts in a journal, now known as *Meditations*. It was not meant for publication and each "chapter" does not deal with a unified theme. Rather, they are the random thoughts of Marcus. Let us take a detour here to follow how this personal journal came to be preserved and became possibly the best-read Stoic classic.

Upon his death in 180 CE, perhaps a family member, friend or an admirer saved it.[159] We don't know if it was copied and published at that time. There was no mention of the book for another two hundred years when historians referred to Aurelius' "exhortations," without having access to the original work itself.[160] When Justinian banned all pagan philosophies in 529 CE, *Meditations* completely disappeared from public view.

Around 900 CE, Arethas Caesarea, a Byzantine scholar, found the manuscript of the journal. He loved it and copied it and began mentioning it in his letters and other writings. He wrote to Demetrius, Metropolitan of Heraclea, to say he (Arethas) had a copy of *Meditations* in poor shape, which he had recopied, so it could be passed to future generations in its renewed condition.

Then the book disappeared from the public view for another four centuries. Around 1300 CE, quotes from *Meditations* started to appear in different sources. The oldest manuscript currently available is with the Vatican Library.[161] In the West, *Meditations* was not quoted until the 16th century.

In 1559, Xylander (Wilhelm Holzmann) translated *Meditations* into Latin and published it with the (now lost) manuscript. This is the only surviving copy of the work besides the Vaticanus Graecus, which dates from the fourteenth century.[162] It is quite obvious that if these two copies had been lost anytime over the next several years, we would not have had access to this most-read Stoic text.

Given the original was written in Koine Greek and copied and recopied, travelling over the centuries, we can't even be sure how faithful the current versions are to the original manuscript. It is not clear whether the original manuscript was neatly divided into 12 chapters ("books") and whether even the original sequence was preserved.

The book was a favorite of several historical figures and thinkers, such Christina of Sweden, Frederick the Great John Stuart Mill, Matthew Arnold, and Goethe. In modern times, political figures such as Bill Clinton and Wen Jiabao claimed to have been influenced by it.

The death of Marcus

Marcus died at the age of 59 on March 17th 180 CE due to natural causes in Vienna, then known as Vindobona. He was immediately deified and cremated and his ashes were returned to Rome.

Before he died, he gathered many of his friends and asked them to guide his son Commodus (see "The last speech of Marcus Aurelius" elsewhere in this book). When he was near death, he said to those around him,

> Go to the rising sun. I am setting.

We don't know what exactly his last words were, but the following final lines of his *Meditations* may well have been his last words:

> You've lived as a citizen of this great world-city. What is it to you whether it is five or five score years? The laws of the city are fair for one and all. What is your complaint?
>
> You are not thrown out of the city by a tyrant or by an unfair judge, but by nature that brought you here in the first place. Like a director dismisses an actor.
>
> "But I have played only three acts of the five."
>
> "Yes, you say it well, but the play has only three acts in your life."
>
> The completeness of the play is decided by the creator of the play. He decides how it ends. These are not your decisions. Make your exit graciously with a smile, with the creator smiling as you exit.

The legacy of Marcus Aurelius

Marcus Aurelius was judged to be one of the "five good emperors" of Rome. (All five good emperors came after some of the worst emperors like Nero, Caligula, and Domitian and none of them had any hereditary claim to royalty.)

He was hailed as a philosopher-king while alive. He is still considered a philosopher-king, probably the most famous of all philosopher-kings.

Marcus always tried to do what he thought was his duty, even when he did not personally like it. He was forgiving of his enemies. He took particular interest in three areas: the freeing of slaves, the guardianship of orphans and minors, and the choosing of city councilors.

From his early teens, Marcus wanted to be a philosopher, yet he became an emperor. Even now, he is remembered as both a good emperor and the author of one of the most loved books on Stoic philosophy.

His biggest mistake was to name his son, Commodus, as his successor. Commodus turned out to be dictatorial.

Historian Herodian best summarized the essence of this philosopher-king:

> *Alone of the emperors, he gave proof of his learning not by mere words or knowledge of philosophical doctrines but by his blameless character and temperate way of life.*[163]

NOTES

1 C.R. Haines. *Marcus Cornelius Fronto: Correspondence Vol. I.* Loeb Classical Library, 1919

2 Amy Richlin. *Marcus Aurelius in Love.* The University of Chicago Press, 2006

3 Robin Hard. *Marcus Aurelius Meditations.* Oxford University Press, 2011.

4 Caillan Davenport and Jennifer Manley, *Fronto: Selected Letters*, Bloomsbury Academic, 2013. (This is a particularly lucid translation with extensive commentaries.)

5 This could refer to the time when there were rumors that Marcus Aurelius' wife was faithful to him while he was away.

6 Probably Herodes Atticus, one of Marcus' teachers.

7 Commodus was about 19 years old around this time.

8 The codex that Mai found was incomplete, containing gaps and jumbled pages. The chemicals that Mai used also had the effect of erasing the original writing. It is quite possible that many gaps and illegible writings were substituted with conjectures by Mai and others after him.

⁹ See, for example, Caillan Davenport and Jennifer Manley, *Fronto: Selected Letters*, Bloomsbury Academic, 2013.

¹⁰ This could refer to his mother or to his wife, but in this case, probably to his mother.

¹¹ An expression based on the myth of Tenedos, meaning unwavering determination.

¹² Second century BCE Roman historian who wrote a history of the Second Punic War, involving considerable bloodshed.

¹³ It is unclear what speech Marcus is referring to here.

¹⁴ Possibly Lorium, where Pius had a villa.

¹⁵ The previous sentence implies his mother Lucilla was away. So, this must refer to Faustina, wife of Pius.

¹⁶ One of the two camps of Latin style, Atticists were known for their ornate style while the other camp, Asianists, preferred a terse and severe style.

¹⁷ Dion was an adolescent from Syracuse when he met Plato. He was considered an eromenos (an adolescent in an erotic relationship with an older man) of Plato.

¹⁸ Off Naples.

¹⁹ Probably Marcus' mother.

²⁰ Troy, located in modern Turkey.

²¹ The god of health worshipped by Pius and Marcus.

²² Presumably Jupiter, whose temple was in the Capitoline Hill in Rome.

²³ The villa owned by Antoninus Pius in Etruria.

---

[24] Marcus never explicitly identifies the trial. Most likely it is the trial of Herodes Atticus, a Greek aristocrat, Roman senator and scholar. The trial was brought by Athenians who sued for the money he owed them according to the terms of his father's will.

[25] Herodes Atticus.

[26] His maternal grandfather.

[27] Some text is missing here.

[28] Probably Salvius Julianus, the renowned jurist.

[29] Probably Quintus Ennius, one of the Roman writers of the second century BCE.

[30] "Driven under the yoke" refers to a ceremony in which defeated soldiers were made to march under a wooden yoke (Amy Richlin, 2006).

[31] Lucius Volucius Maecianus, one of Marcus Aurelius' teachers.

[32] Quintus Cornelius Quadratus.

[33] Probably refers to a lost work by Sotades.

[34] Gaius Sempronius Gracchus, a second century BCE Roman orator, with a vehement style.

[35] The word possibly means "to cool down" (C.R. Haines, 1919).

[36] Amy Richlin points out that what is referred to here as a letter could have been one of Marcus' books.

[37] A notebook kept by Fronto entitled *Exempla Elocutionum* containing excerpts from Terence, Vergil, Cicero and Sallust.

[38] According to C.R. Haines, Marcus did not receive the title Imperator until 147 and was not styled so until 161. Therefore, there must be some error here.

[39] The illness referred to here is gout or arthritis.

[40] Mineral baths or hot springs.

[41] The reference is to Fronto's *Pro Somno* (For Sleep).

[42] Probably refers to Ulysses being driven back and forth along the coast.

[43] *Odyssey*, 31, Tr. C.R. Haines.

[44] *Odyssey*, 29, Tr. C.R. Haines.

[45] *Odyssey*, 46, Tr. C.R. Haines.

[46] *Odyssey*, xii.338, Tr. C.R. Haines.

[47] *Odyssey*, xi.108, Tr. C.R. Haines.

[48] *Odyssey*, xii.370, 372, Tr. C.R. Haines.

[49] *Odyssey*, i.58.

[50] *Odyssey*, iv.22,23.

[51] *Odyssey*, ii.24.

[52] Refers to Fronto.

[53] Hesiod, *Theog.* 22f (from C.R. Haines' notes).

[54] Odessey, xiii.80.

[55] Possibly *De Virtue*, according to C.R. Haines.

[56] This is C.R. Haines' Loeb version. The codex attributes the quote to Thucydides (see Amy Richlin, 2006).

[57] Fronto's wife.

[58] Roman comic playwright who lived around the second/third century BCE.

[59] Roman writer, second century BCE.

[60] The Emperor Marcus Antoninus Pius, Marcus' adoptive father.

[61] Antoninus Pius.

[62] A junior magistrate assigned to Fronto, possibly Victorinus or Fronto's brother Quadratus.

[63] Roman Orator and statesman, 2nd century BCE.

[64] Rhetorician, 2nd Century BCE.

[65] Hendecasyllable = 11 syllables (the previous clause in Latin follows this metrical pattern).

[66] Marcus Aurelius' name at this time was known as Marcus Annius Verus.

[67] It is unclear whether this and the next letter refer to the thanks for Fronto's consulship. If they did, Pius would have given Fronto the title (see C.R. Haines, 1919).

[68] Probably, this refers to the younger daughter of Pius.

[69] The desolate Aegean Island to which banished people are sent.

[70] The elder Cato.

[71] The emperor, Antoninus Pius.

[72] Greek sculptor, 5th Century BCE.

[73] Greek painter, 4th Century BCE.

[74] Greek orator, 4th Century BCE.

[75] Fronto was influenced by the style of early Latin writers.

[76] Marcus is aware of his weakness and does not fear admonition, because he needs it.

[77] Marcus appears to be referring to himself.

[78] The earliest national poet of Rome.

[79] A line of verse that has six metrical feet, usually all in the same or a related meter. The Greek and Latin poems "The Iliad," "The Odyssey," and "The Aeneid" are composed in hexameters.

[80] Probably refers to Augustan poet, orator and historian (C.R. Haines).

[81] July and August, the two months of Fronto's consulship, when Fronto had to be in Rome.

[82] Roman comic playwright, first century BCE.

[83] Writers of formal praises.

[84] Historian and orator (3rd century BCE).

[85] Caecilius Statius, Roman comic poet (2nd century BCE).

[86] Marcus Porcius, Cato.

[87] Masurius Sabinus, law professor (1st century BCE), known for his long-winded text.

[88] Fronto's wife.

[89] The daughter of Fronto, named after her mother.

[90] The elder Cato.

[91] Sallust, the historian.

[92] Pius' villa, twelve miles from Rome, where he died.

[93] The Emperor Antoninus Pius.

[94] Extract fro***

[95] Title of a Roman priest.

[96] One of the people of Latium, around Rome.

[97] Around the Via Aurelia.

[98] Around the Bay of Naples.

[99] Pun of the word that means both "run through" and "read."

[100] This expression means "looking for good wine."

[101] Known for its medicinal grapes.

[102] Nothing is known about this speech.

[103] Built by Augustus, 28BCE.

[104] In the palace of Tiberius.

[105] Meaning "fit to be destroyed."

[106] A phrase from a comedy. Marcus rejects the word "gargle," a Greek word Latinized as a medical term (source: Amy Richlin. *Marcus in Love*).

[107] Antoninus Pius, the emperor.

[108] Probably full of fish eggs.

[109] From the poet Novius, mentioned earlier.

[110] Fronto's wife.

[111] Fronto's daughter.

[112] Not known who is referred to here.

[113] First mention of Faustina in connection with Marcus whom she married in 145CE.

[114] Homer.

[115] It is not known what misfortune of Fronto Marcus Aurelius is referring to.

[116] Annia Cornificia, born around 123 CE.

[117] This would be Lorium, somewhere in the country.

[118] It is not clear whether Marcus is referring to Faustina or to his mother.

[119] Annia Galeria Faustina, born probably in 146 CE and died in infancy.

[120] Apparently his daughter in this context.

¹²¹ Note that by this time, Marcus has dropped his long affectionate salutations. From here on, almost all Marcus' letters to Fronto start with "To my master," and end with "Goodbye, the best/delightful of my masters."

¹²² Victorinus, friend of Marcus Aurelius and the future son-in-law of Fronto.

¹²³ Stoic philosopher of the third century BCE, a student of Zeno and a contemporary Chrysippus.

¹²⁴ Possibly Plautus.

¹²⁵ Considered to be a very important statement. By saying that he could no longer defend both sides of an argument, Marcus rejects rhetoric in preference to philosophy. Rusticus and philosophy definitely win over Fronto and rhetoric.

¹²⁶ Probably his wife Faustina. Marcus married her in 145 CE.

¹²⁷ Annia Galeria Faustina and Annia Lucilla, who was born around 148 CE.

¹²⁸ Refers to Asia. Fronto was consul in 143, and then proconsul.

¹²⁹ Here, Marcus is referring to Fronto's severe illness. We don't know the details of the disease.

¹³⁰ This is in response to Fronto's observation that he loved Marcus ten times as much after seeing his daughter who resembled him and Faustina.

¹³¹ This is not what Fronto actually said though.

¹³² Marcus' birthday.

¹³³ This is in response to Fronto's complaint about his stomach pains and diarrhea.

¹³⁴ Marcus' mother Lucilla, who died in 156 CE. This is her last mention by Marcus.

¹³⁵ The great-aunt of Marcus.

¹³⁶ Lucilla and Fadilla.

¹³⁷ The both were *pantomime*.

¹³⁸ Probably a freedman of Verus, named after a great actor.

¹³⁹ Twenty-four miles from Rome, on the Etrurian Coast.

¹⁴⁰ Halfway between Alsium and Rome.

¹⁴¹ Likely his daughter Cornificia.

¹⁴² Likely Cornificia.

¹⁴³ A play on words.

¹⁴⁴ Antoninus Geminus and Lucius Aurelius Commodus were born on August 31.

¹⁴⁵ Victorinus, who married Gratia around 160 CE.

¹⁴⁶ Lucius Verus who, by this time, was away leading the Parthian war.

¹⁴⁷ He playfully refers to the letter as the "speech."

¹⁴⁸ Lucius Verus, his colleague.

¹⁴⁹ From the defeat of Xerxes to the Peloponnesian War.

¹⁵⁰ Although Fronto sends a sketchy draft in reply, the fuller account of the wars was probably never written owing to Fronto's death in 166 or 167 CE.

¹⁵¹ There are those who believe his name could have been (at birth or later) Marcus Annius Catilius Severus or Marcus Catilius Severus Annius Verus.

¹⁵² Strictly speaking, it was probably Apollonius Chalcedon who introduced Marcus to Stoicism. However, Marcus was greatly influenced by Rusticus.

[153] *Meditations*, I.7 (Tr. Gregory Hayes).

[154] *Meditations*, VI.30.

[155] Second only to the king, the *tribunician* is the commander of the king's personal bodyguard, with the authority to pass laws.

[156] Power to command.

[157] Chief high priest of the College of Pontiffs in ancient Rome.

[158] Eastern and central part of modern Switzerland.

[159] Hadot, Pierre (1998) *Inner Citadel*. Harvard.

[160] Eg. Historia Augusta, referred to by Hadot (1998) above.

[161] Vaticanus Graecus 1950

[162] The story of *Meditations* described here has been based on two sources: Pierre Hadot (1998) above and Marcel van Ackeren. *A Companion to Marcus Aurelius* (2012).

[163] Herodian, *Ab Excessu Divi Marci*, 1.2.4 (Tr. Echols; source: Wikipedia).

ABOUT THE AUTHOR

Dr. Chuck Chakrapani has been a long-term, but embarrassingly inconsistent, practitioner of Stoicism. He is the president of Leger Analytics, Chief Knowledge Officer of The Blackstone Group in Chicago, and a Distinguished Visiting Professor at Ryerson University.

Chuck has written books on several subjects over the years, which include research methods, statistics, and investment strategies. His personal website is Chuck-Chakrapani.com

His books on Stoicism include *Unshakable Freedom, A Fortunate Storm,* and *The Good Life Handbook* (a rendering of Epictetus' *Enchiridion.*)

ALSO BY THE AUTHOR

A Fortunate Storm

Three unconnected events – a shipwreck in Piraeus, a play in Thebes, and the banishment of a rebel in Turkey – connected three unrelated individuals to give birth to a philosophy that was to endure 2,000 years.

Get a FREE COPY of the eBook at TheStoicGym.com

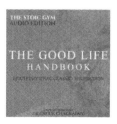

The Good Life Handbook

Available in print, digital, and audio editions, *The Good Life Handbook* is a rendering of *Enchiridion* in plain English.

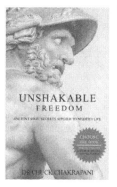

Unshakable Freedom

How can we achieve total personal freedom when we have so many obligations and so many demands on our time? Is personal freedom even possible?

Yes, it is possible, said the Stoics.

162

Stoicism in Plain English

Stoicism in Plain English books 1-5 represent the complete works of Epictetus.

Stoic Foundations (Discourses Book 1) explains the basic tenets of Stoicism.

Stoic Choices is the plain English version of Discourses Book 2. It revolves around themes of choice.

Stoic Training is the third book of *Discourses* of Epictetus in plain English. Stoics did not only believe in theoretical knowledge but held that it is critical we practice what we learned.

Stoic Freedom (Discourses Book 4) focuses on freedom. Personal freedom is close to Epictetus' heart, and his rhetoric shines when he talks about freedom. But, what does a free person look like?

Stoic Inspirations combines the Enchiridion (Epictetus' pupil Arrian's notebook summarizing his teachings) and the remaining fragments of the lost Discourses books. It completes the Stoicism in Plain English series on Epictetus from The Stoic Gym.

Musonius Rufus' Stoic Lessons

Stoic Lessons is the complete works of Musonius Rufus (25-95CE), the man who taught Epictetus. While he was very well-known and respected during his time, he is less widely known now. He was a social activist, a proto-feminist, a vegetarian, and a minimalist.

The Complete Works of Marcus Aurelius

Meditations by Emperor Marcus Aurelius (121-180 CE) is probably the most beloved, uplifting, and widely read classic of Stoic philosophy.

Marcus ruled the greatest empire the world had seen up until his time. Yet he faced several problems, both personal and political.

Glimpse the private man behind the public persona.

Marcus Aurelius the Unknown completes The Stoic Gym's Plain English rendition of the most popular stoic's complete works.

Get your copies in your favorite online bookstore.

164

Made in the USA
Middletown, DE
16 January 2019